# Abnormal Psychology
# An International
# Perspective

# Abnormal Psychology
# An International Perspective

Jennie Brooks Jamison, M.Ed.

*Abnormal Psychology: An International Perspective* is meant to inform and educate teachers and students about a wide range of psychological theories and research investigating mental health and ways to improve mental health with an international minded approach. The materials provided are meant for information purposes and are not meant as medical advice or instructions. *Abnormal Psychology: An International Perspective* is not to be used for self-diagnosis and treatment for any mental health, physical health, or general well-being concern. Please consult a licensed physician or other health care provider about all mental health, physical health, or well-being concerns and discuss anything of interest from this book with that person.

"International Baccalaureate" is a registered trademark of the International Baccalaureate Organization (IB). The material in this text has been developed independently of the IB, which was not involved with the production of this text and in no way endorses it.

© 2013 Wisdom Quest, LLC

ISBN-13: 978-1492137030
ISBN-10: 1492137030

All Rights Reserved

Printed in the United States of America

# About the Author

Jennie Brooks Jamison has been teaching International Baccalaureate (IB) psychology since 1986 at St. Petersburg High School in Florida. Jennie leads workshops for both new and experienced IB psychology teachers and is an experienced examiner for the Internal Assessment and Paper 1.

*Abnormal Psychology: An International Perspective* is Jennie's fifth book.

Jennie actively practices Tai Chi, Yoga and P90X, is establishing a small urban farm with her husband, rescues cats, hikes the Florida Everglades and the Blue Ridge Mountains whenever possible, and lives St. Petersburg, Florida.


Also by Jennie Brooks Jamison:
Understanding Research Methods in Psychology:
    Second Edition (2013)
Health Psychology: Where East Meets West in Perfect
    Balance (2012)
Levels of Analysis in Psychology (2010)

# Acknowledgements
I am indebted to Jamie Barnes for giving her opinions on the book and helping with editing.

# Contents

Preface   p. 12

## Chapter 1   p. 13
### Introduction
The future of global mental health— Stress, an interactive approach, and culture— Defining mental disorders

## Chapter 2   p. 19
### Examine the concepts of normality and abnormality
Normality and abnormality: The elements of abnormality— Allan Horwitz's concerns about the changing definitions of abnormality—Arthur Kleinman's concerns about DSM-5 expansion of abnormality—Theory of Knowledge Link— Culture, normality, and abnormality

## Chapter 3   p. 28
### Discuss validity and reliability of diagnosis
Can we end automatic reifying?—Positive and negative aspects of diagnosis—Setting the stage for discussing reliability and validity— A brief history of the DSM and ICD— The first classification systems—DSM I & II— DSM III & IV— DSM-5

## Chapter 4  p. 38
### Discuss cultural and ethical considerations in diagnosis
What is important to consider about culture and the validity of diagnosis?—Classification of eating disorders: A specific example of the concern and positive changes— Etics/emics overview—Cultural syndromes— To what extent are Uganda's Baganda depressed in a western sense?—Eclectic treatments: Combining local healing with western treatments to satisfy needs of local communities

## Chapter 5  p. 52
### Describe symptoms and prevalence of major depression: The example for affective disorders
DSM-5 diagnosis for major depression, prevalence reports, and culture related diagnostic issues— CCMD-3 diagnosis for depressive episode—Prevalence of depression in China

## Chapter 6  p. 62
### Describe symptoms and prevalence of anorexia nervosa (AN): The example for eating disorders
DSM-5 diagnosis for anorexia nervosa (AN)— CCMD-3 diagnosis for anorexia nervosa— Prevalence rates of anorexia in nonwestern countries

## Chapter 7  p. 68
### Analyze etiologies of two mental disorders: Major depression
A frame of reference for considering depression—A list of factors that increase the risk of depression—Biological

level of analysis: Background ideas for understanding genes and depression— Biological level of analysis: Human genetic studies about 5-HTT and depression— Biological level of analysis: Animal genetic research— Biological level of analysis: The dimensions of culture and gene expression—Cognitive level of analysis: The theory about cognitive style and depressive schemas— Cognitive level of analysis: Two studies showing that cognition is a risk factor for depression— Sociocultural level of analysis: Techno-brain burnout: Internet use, stress, and depression — Sociocultural level of analysis: Theory of Knowledge Link—Sociocultural level of analysis: Two studies about Internet use and depression

## Chapter 8 p. 89
## Analyze etiologies of two mental disorders: Anorexia nervosa (AN)

A list of factors that increase the risk of AN— Biological level of analysis: Genetic factors— Cognitive level of analysis: Research about cognitive style— Cognitive level of analysis: A second cognitive style study— Sociocultural level of analysis: Media— Sociocultural level of analysis: A second media study

## Chapter 9 p. 102
## Discuss cultural and gender variations in prevalence of disorders

Why is it hard to know about culture and prevalence?—A World Health Organization (WHO) survey about culture and prevalence—Background concepts for considering gender variations in prevalence of mental disorders— Gender variations in prevalence of depression— Gender variations in prevalence of eating disorders— Two survey studies about gender and culture differences in prevalence of eating disorders in the U.S.

## Chapter 10  p. 116
## Examine biomedical, individual, and group approaches to treatment
Assumptions of a biomedical approach to treatment— Assumptions of an individual approach to treatment— Assumptions of a group approach to treatment

## Chapter 11  p. 121
## Examine the use of biomedical, individual, and group approaches to the treatment of one disorder: Major depression
Background for understanding depression treatments— A cross-cultural list of depression treatments— Biomedical treatments— Individual treatments—Group treatments— Some things to consider when evaluating treatments— Biomedical treatment #1: The antidepressant Prozac—The case of Lauren Slater—Thinking about Prozac— Prozac treatment for adolescents: The 3 TADS studies about Prozac and their combination with cognitive therapy— Prozac normalizes the brain— Culture and antidepressants: The example of Japan— Biomedical treatment #2: Exercise is just as effective as drugs— Exercise helps maintain depression treatment— Biomedical treatment #3: Acupuncture is an effective depression treatment— Two acupuncture experiments— Individual treatment: Cognitive therapy (CT)— Cognitive therapy study #1: CT is effective for severely depressed patients— Cognitive therapy study #2: CT and antidepressants target different symptoms— Culture and cognitive therapy for depression— Group treatment: Mindfulness-based cognitive therapy (MBCT)—

Group treatment: A cross-cultural experiment about group interpersonal therapy (IPT) with adolescent war survivors

## Chapter 12  p. 154
## Discuss the use of eclectic approaches to treatment
Advantages of using an eclectic approach— Limitations of using an eclectic approach— Eclectic example #1: Antidepressants and cognitive therapy for depression— Eclectic example #2: Antidepressants and acupuncture for depression

## Chapter 13  p. 157
## Discuss the relationship between etiology and therapeutic approach to one disorder

## Chapter 14  p. 160
## To what extent do biological, cognitive, and sociocultural factors influence abnormal behavior?
Examples of the influence

## Chapter 15  p. 162
## Evaluate psychological research relevant to the study of abnormal behavior
Guiding points for evaluating research

## References p. 164

# Preface

Revising chapter 7 from the first edition of *Levels of Analysis in Psychology* into a separate book was the right thing to do as I considered the changes to the discipline and insights into teaching IB that had occurred since the first edition that follow.
1. DSM-5 is new and offers both positive changes and difficult challenges going forward. These changes affect material from many learning outcomes.
2. Research about etiology changes quickly and the newest research emphasizes an integrative approach.
3. New treatment research clarifies when and in what combination to use treatments. More cultural practices are now combined with western treatment!
4. Abnormal psychology is a popular topic. This book weaves critical thinking into the discussion, aiming for the highest marks.
5. More links to Paper 1 topics are now available, including genetics, evolutionary explanations of behavior, neurotransmission, effects of the environment on physiology, schemas, etics/emics, and the dimensions of culture.
6. More links to Theory of Knowledge are required and example questions for discussion are included in this book.

I recommend reading the book with your class. Let class discussions naturally emerge from the reading.

# Chapter 1
# Introduction

## The future of global mental health

We have the power to significantly reduce mental illness. While there are no simple answers to why people get mental disorders and what to do about them, creating a sense of empowerment to bring well-being to all is the goal. The IB mission focuses on **internationalism** and a **learner profile** that includes developing caring, knowledgeable, principled, and reflective people. A course with a cross-cultural perspective is a clear path to stimulating intellectual growth, **intercultural understanding**, and compassion.

Let's consider the scope of mental illness on a global scale. Over 450 million people worldwide have a mental illness (Torgovnick, 2012). Mental disorders account for more than 13% of global disease, consisting mainly of depression, substance use disorder, and schizophrenia. By 2030, mental illness is projected to become the second greatest health disease burden in middle-income countries and the third highest in low-income countries. Contrary to popular belief, people in rich countries do not always have access to mental health care. Nearly 50% of people living in rich countries with a diagnosed mental illness do not get treatment, and it escalates to 90% in low-income nations. People with mental health problems are less productive than they could be and have a greater risk of additional health problems.

Adolescent mental health prevalence is also a concern because untreated early mental disorder affects all aspects of development (Patel, Flisher, Hetrick, & McGorry, 2007). "At least one out of every four to five young people in the general population will suffer from at least one mental disorder in any given year" (p. 1303).

The current global scope is no improvement over a previous World Health Report (2001) warning, "One person in four will be affected by a mental disorder at some stage of life" (p.1). The World Health Organization (WHO) Director-General speculated that major depression was the leading cause of disability globally and had the potential to become a major cause of disease. The warnings may be a current reality.

With all that modern medicine offers to treat mental illness, why is the problem growing? Could the benefits of modernization and globalization also come with increased stress that contributes to mental disorder?

I will not leave you without hope. Mental health care advocate Vickram Patel suggests in a TED talk that mental health care can be delivered in ways that empower local communities (Torgovnick, 2012). Severe shortages of psychiatrists exist, with estimates of ratios as great as 1 to 200,000 people in some countries. Many do not have access to care even in rich countries. Patel suggests that more people can be trained to deliver basic mental health services, such as local nurses and other community health care providers. Patel gave the example of an Ugandan program where villagers were trained to give psychotherapy and 90% of people receiving the therapy improved. Somehow we can come together to promote well-being in our communities!

## Stress, an interactive approach, and culture

Three themes have emerged in the field of abnormal psychology over the years that form a foundation for reflecting on mental disorders.

First, reducing **stress** lowers the risk of mental illness. Stress contributes to all mental illness, even the disorders students most associate with genetics, such as schizophrenia and autism. The genetic contribution to schizophrenia is about 50%, leaving room for other factors, such as stress. Twins are not 100% concordant for autism, so sociocultural factors must place stress on the developing brain. Understanding the role of stress in mental illness affects decisions about treatments and shifts the emphasis to creating health. Genetic contributions to substance use disorders are about 50%, and we now know that most genes related to mental illnesses, including depression and anorexia, can unfold in specific environments. We have control over the environment and can take action if educated.

Second, the many factors contributing to mental illness are vast and interact. The **bidirectional model** shows how some factors important for the course interact and reduces oversimplification. The model is a modern view of **diathesis-stress**, meaning a predisposition for a disorder. Historical views of diathesis were reductionist, often focusing on biological diatheses, such as genes. We now know that diathesis is a mixture of factors that interact, such as stressful life events and their effects on gene expression. The model is most useful for understanding two IB learning outcomes, etiologies, or factors contributing to mental illness, and how biological, cognitive, and sociocultural factors influence abnormal behavior.

**Sociocultural factors**, such as cultural values, media, and Internet overuse

**Cognitive factors**, such as cognitive style, rumination, and cognitive inflexibility

**Biological factors**, such as genes, neurotransmitters, and chi (energy) imbalance

General Bidirectional Model

Third, an international view is recommended. While the IB syllabus has two specific headings for "culture and diagnosis" and "culture and prevalence," all the material is best organized under culture. *Otherwise, I am afraid students will approach mental illness with the frame of reference of their own cultures, looking at cultural differences as variations of the "real" way to view mental disorder.*

A more realistic approach focuses on **cognitive schemas**, or beliefs about a group's experiences with behavior (Castillo, 1997). Cognitive schemas **reify** beliefs into something real for the group. Reifying "occurs when people are collectively projecting onto an object a level of reality the object does not really possess" (p. 19). The way a behavior is thought of in a cultural group is real to them, even if it is not in actuality real. The brain adapts to the cultural schemas and the group treats a set of behaviors as real mental illnesses. Do not assume that others outside of your culture share similar schemas.

How do schemas about mental illness form? Specific behavior is noticed by a cultural group and is interpreted as a mental illness within a cultural definition. The cultural definition becomes the reality. This is why, for example, the group of symptoms called "depression" in the West are not always accepted in other cultures.

## Defining mental disorders

Classifying mental disorders in the Diagnostic and Statistical Manual for Mental Disorders (**DSM-5**) and the International Classification of Disease (**ICD-10**) is *evolving*. DSM-5 arrived in 2013 and the ICD-11 will be available by 2015. Although other cultures have similar diagnostic systems that developed in line with western manuals, such as the Chinese Classification of Mental Disorder (**CCMD-3**), the systems retain culture specific features useful for their populations.

Strategies to define cultural variations of mental disorders are moving forward. DSM-5 includes a new Cultural Formulation Interview (CFI) to make diagnosis culturally relevant, an advance over previous manuals. However, DSM-5 instructs that health providers *may use* the CFI to clarify cultural situations. Its use is not required, but is an advancement. The IB mission statement focuses on internationalism, and with all we know about culture and mental illness, the DSM-5 change is helpful.

Defining any mental disorder is challenging. Psychologists now understand that mental disorder results from the complex interplay between biology, cognitions, and sociocultural factors. In addition, no definite and clear distinction exists between mental health and mental disorder. DSM-IV (2000) even included the statement, "There is no assumption that each category of mental disorder is a complete discrete entity with absolute boundaries dividing it from other mental disorders or from no mental disorder" (p. xxxi). However, DSM-IV required health providers to use a rigid diagnostic categories that were not always a clear fit.

DSM-5 still organizes mental illness into categories. Increasing **reliability** and stimulating research are its main purposes. DSM-5 does try to fix some DSM-IV limitations. One example is severity ratings for each disorder to provide some flexibility so real clinical cases have a chance to fit with diagnosis.

Depression and Anorexia Nervosa are the example disorders used to explore abnormal psychology concepts.

# Chapter 2

## Examine the concepts of normality and abnormality

### Normality and abnormality: The elements of abnormality

There is no agreed upon definition of "**normality**" and "**abnormality**." Although some behaviors are clearly outside of accepted norms for any culture, such as schizophrenia and autism, others are debatable, such as the group of symptoms called depression in western societies.

When teaching it is important to avoid vagueness and oversimplification by using the elements of abnormality to distinguish the concepts and flesh out important issues.

The six **elements of abnormality** are useful for judging the difference between normal and abnormal behavior (Butcher, Mineka, & Hooley, 2007). One element may not be enough to make someone abnormal. The risk of abnormality increases with each addition of an element. Consider what each factor means and get some working examples for discussion, such as the one below about Sherri Souza.

1. Suffering
2. Maladaptiveness
3. Deviancy

4. Violation of the standards of society
5. Social discomfort
6. Irrationality and unpredictability

Note to the teacher:

> For a class activity, students consider the meaning of each item and rank them in order of importance, noting that one is not necessarily enough to call someone abnormal or mentally ill. We have a discussion where students defend their responses and challenge each other, citing examples of disorders.

The case of Sherri Souza, whose spouse's return from military service in Iraq was postponed longer than expected for an extra tour of duty, is a good example (Horwitz, 2005). Sherri's symptoms included missing her husband, feeling anxiety for his safety, feeling anxiety over how her family would fare if he was killed or seriously injured, experiencing distress over late e-mails, and hiding in bed to wait for news.

Do Sherri's symptoms make her abnormal? Sherri described herself as depressed and was prescribed antidepressants. What do you think? *How many elements does Sherri have?* The answer is important and reflects your culture's **schemas** about normal and abnormal. The schemas of one's culture affect what is diagnosed as a mental illness, so the learning outcomes about normality and abnormality and validity and reliability of diagnosis are closely tied.

Allan Horwitz and Arthur Kleinman are two theorists highlighting concerns about defining normality and abnormality. Both worry that definitions of "abnormal" have expanded too much over time, with many consequences for people.

Schemas about normal and abnormal change over time, and affect diagnosing mental illness. The fifth edition of the Diagnostic and Statistical Manual for Mental Disorder (DSM-5) was released in 2013, illustrating a new chapter in thinking about normal and abnormal. Each edition of the DSM has refined, thrown out, and created new categories of mental disorder based on assumptions about normal and abnormal.

Overall, each DSM is more inclusive for many disorders, such as depression. This means that more people are considered abnormal and meet the diagnosis.

Some definitions of abnormal disappear or merge with other listed disorders with each manual, and previous abnormal behavior is now normal or must be reclassified as abnormal in a different way. For example, Aspergers' is no longer a disorder in DSM-5. Autism spectrum disorder is a new diagnosis meant to consolidate several DSM-IV disorders, including Aspergers'. Critics wonder how many people with Aspergers' will qualify. Whether it is a good development depends on whom you ask.

## Allan Horwitz's concerns about changing definitions of abnormality

Horwitz (2005) writes that serious mental illness needs diagnosis and treatment, but believes some groups of symptoms have become *over-pathologized*, such as "depressive" symptoms, except when someone has severe depression with suicidal thoughts and/or psychotic symptoms. Horwitz raised questions a long time ago about the **validity** of the DSM-IV diagnosis for major depression and wondered if changing assumptions about "normality" and "abnormality" had turned everyday unhappiness into a disorder.

Note to the teacher:

> Horwitz's article, *The Age of Depression*, is free on the Internet and is recommended for teachers because it details the evolution of the DSM from DSM-I to DSM-IV.

The first two editions of DSM were context sensitive, meaning abnormality was diagnosed according to an individual's life situation. Horwitz examines the history of thinking about normal and abnormal using depression as an example. Early thought, including Freudian theory, distinguished depression *"without a cause,"* where the person was depressed even though everything in their life was fine, and depression *"with cause,"* meaning something happened to the person, such as a family death. The term, **bereavement exclusion** comes from the distinction, meaning people grieving a loss were not treated for depression, but instead had depression-like symptoms "with cause." Only depression "without a cause" was considered abnormal. DSM I and II reflected the distinction. However, if abnormality was judged within the context of someone's life circumstances, it made diagnosis unreliable; it was too hard for everyone to talk about the same thing.

Students familiar with Rosenhan's (1973) observation study, where people posed as mentally ill to gain admission to hospitals, know that the failure of hospital personnel to distinguish normal from abnormal shook the psychiatric community. The controversy was one factor prompting the change to a symptom-based DSM in 1980. Rosenhan's study is free on the Internet and popular with students.

DSM III and IV focused on symptom lists all could agree upon to increase **reliability**, where people were considered abnormal, or depressed, if they had a certain number of the symptoms (Horwitz, 2005). No longer was a theory about causation based on life situations necessary. In addition, DSM-III changed the distinction between depression "with and without a cause," allowing a depression diagnosis one year after the death of a loved one. DSM-IV further shortened the time to two months.

Horwitz wonders about the trend toward inclusiveness. Consider the issue in a class discussion. Does including more people as depressed help people get needed treatment? Are more people inappropriately called abnormal? Did ordinary sadness become abnormal? Does it belittle the situation of people with serious mental illnesses? What societal factors contributed to the changes?

## Arthur Kleinman's concerns about DSM-5 expansion of abnormality

Horwitz's arguments get a new twist with the unveiling of DSM-5. Kleinman (2012) is compassionate and insightful, and he wonders if the changes to diagnosing major depression in DSM-5 have gone too far. DSM-5 removes the bereavement exclusion, allowing someone with symptoms of grief from the death of a loved one, including sadness, disturbed sleep, loss of appetite, and feelings of deep loss, to be labeled abnormal and diagnosed as depression after the two-week symptom requirement.

Kleinman's article, *The Art of Medicine*, is free on the Internet and is worth reading. Kleinman wonders if the changes to thinking about normal and abnormal will have profound consequences for people. How long should someone grieve after the death of a close family member? No consensus exists. Every culture has traditions about grieving that vary greatly, up to a lifetime for some, and rules vary according to gender. Is grieving natural, helping people move forward? What would the world look like without grieving? Might the failure to grieve and work through someone's death prolong the symptoms and contribute to long-term problems? Are cultural norms shifting to where feeling bad in any way is unacceptable? How important are unfortunate obstacles for maturing a person over the lifespan?

## Theory of Knowledge Link

TOK lessons about the social sciences can include a discussion about the terms **normal, abnormal**, and **humanness**. Read the Kleinman (2012) article and consider the following questions.

1. To what extent should we end suffering, one element of abnormality? Does possessing the available technology obligate us to end as many elements of abnormality as possible? How does your answer affect conceptions of "humanness"?
2. To what extent is grieving or shyness normal? When should grieving be considered depression and shyness be considered social anxiety?
3. Technology has shaped the younger generations. To what extent do you see the medicalization of grief or shyness as advances?
4. DSM-5 aims to help people. Could we see unintended consequences, such as postponing the inevitable need to grieve, and perhaps make the person's problem worse in the long run? How do we balance the goal to help and a person's need to struggle with life's challenges?
5. Evaluate Kleinman's claim that medicalizing grief is motivated in part by pharmaceutical company profit interests. Consider the counterclaim that potential benefits exist.
6. The terms normal and abnormal change over time and vary by culture. How can we effectively apply the terms?

DSM-5 supporters defend the bereavement exclusion, suggesting some people need a depression diagnosis when symptoms occur at the same time as an important loss (American Psychiatric Association, 2013). "When they occur together, the depressive symptoms and functional impairment tend to be more severe and the prognosis is worse compared with bereavement that is not accompanied by major depressive disorder" (p. 155).

Next is a discussion of culture and abnormality intended to place the elements of abnormality into an international context.

## Culture, normality, and abnormality

A person's cultural context is critical to considering "normality" and "abnormality" (Marsella & Yamada, 2007). The issue is closely tied to cultural considerations in diagnosis. Culture complicates thinking about normality and abnormality, but a diagnosis without it is incomplete (Marsella & Yamada, 2007).

Understanding a person's cultural construction of reality helps us avoid calling them abnormal when they are not and conversely, helps us understand when someone is really abnormal and needs treatment. Otherwise, there is a risk of over or under-diagnosing people and giving destructive treatments.

Almost every culture has its own system of diagnosis (Marsella & Yamada, 2007). Although the Chinese Classification of Mental Disorders (**CCMD-3**) is a good example of a nonwestern classification system, it is not the only alternative to the **DSM-5** and the **ICD-10**. Other diagnostic systems appear similar to western classification systems to some degree, but do not assume they are the same (Marsella & Yamada, 2007). For example, the meaning of the word depression is different for ethnic Pakistani living in the U.K. than it is for western psychiatrists, affecting diagnosis and treatment expectations (Tabassum, 2000). Pakistani views on abnormality are related to physical behaviors, such as aggression. Western views revolve around emotions. Misunderstandings are easy to imagine.

Avoid **decontextualizing** disorders (Marsella & Yamada, 2007). A disorder is not automatically similar for another culture. For example, **susto** is a way for some people in Mexican, Central American, and South American cultures to show distress (American Psychiatric Association, 2013). Susto's cause is the soul leaving the body during a stressful event. Symptoms include sleep difficulties, withdrawal, loss of appetite, and listlessness. Treatment for susto can include rituals using meditations, passing chicken eggs over the body, and herbs. The symptoms of Susto are similar to western depression. Is susto a depressive disorder? *Do any similarities mean the disorder shares the same causes, expression and course as those in the West?* Absolutely not! "How can we separate a disorder from the very psyche in which it is construed and the very social context in which people respond to it" (Marsella & Yamada, 2007, p. 807-808)?

# Chapter 3

## Discuss validity and reliability of diagnosis

### Can we end automatic reifying?
Students frequently believe that mental disorders are real things. It is the biggest challenge for teaching abnormal psychology. *Reifying is automatic unless teachers make a big deal about it.* Reifying means to make an abstract idea real. Even the DSM-IV-TR (2000) warned, "A common misconception is that a classification system of mental disorders classifies people, when really what are being classified are disorders that people have" (p. xxxi). A more productive approach is to think about people "meeting the criteria for major depression" than to say, "the depressed person." In addition, cultural **schemas** affect the expression and course of mental illness, so mental illnesses are not always the same thing across cultures. All diagnostic systems are the result of cultural schemas about normal and abnormal.

The following situations may help reduce reifying.

If a person reports symptoms such as blurry vision, itchy skin, cuts and sores healing slowly, increased thirst, frequent urination, and leg pain, a doctor thinks, "This person may have diabetes." The doctor sends the person for a blood test to verify if diabetes is the correct diagnosis.

Physical disorders are "things" and have lab tests to verify the diagnoses.

Does it make sense to diagnose a fever by asking the patient to state how he or she feels? Would you take the person's temperature instead?

In contrast, if someone reports symptoms such as sadness, difficulty sleeping, feelings of worthlessness, decreased appetite and thoughts of suicide, a doctor thinks, "This person may have major depression." The doctor cannot order a blood test to confirm the suspicion. Questionnaires measuring subjective self-reports, often administered by health providers, are used to make the diagnosis. Biological, cognitive, and sociocultural markers for mental disorders are still in developmental stages, though some exist. To compliment matters, some people may seem "crazy" but are really just expressing behavior that is part of their culture.

## Positive and negative aspects of diagnosis

The unveiling of **DSM-5** is a good time to consider the strengths and limitations of diagnostic systems. Just remember that no classification system is "right" because they change over time and are not the only way to describe a person's symptoms.

Classifying disorders has advantages and disadvantages. On the positive side, health professionals can all talk about the same thing. In addition, researchers can study disorders more easily using participants fitting into a diagnostic category. On the negative side, a diagnosis can become a stigma or a label that prevents someone from taking personal action to improve their situation.

Diagnostic manuals have both supporters and critics.

Supporters claim that DSM-5 transforms diagnosis in many ways, some of which look encouraging. One example was changing the diagnosis of anorexia by eliminating the symptom about having a fear of getting fat, often called the "fat phobia." The fat phobia made diagnosis difficult cross-culturally and even forced many western patients into a vaguer diagnosis of "eating disorders not otherwise specified," which made understanding and treating the disordered eating difficult.

The National Institute of Mental Health (NIMH) is one critic. NIMH is unhappy with DSM-5 for using lists of symptoms for diagnosis rather than biological markers that can be objectively measured, which compromises **validity** (Insel, 2013). Future NIMH research will not focus on DSM-5 mental disorder categories, but will design studies to identify biological and cognitive markers.

The Kleinman (2012) article recommended in the last chapter is important because it outlines some potential problems with over-diagnosing depression.

Note to the teacher:

> Examples of biological markers are increasing. **Cognitive inflexibility** is a potential marker for anorexia, reviewed in chapter 8 about etiologies of anorexia.

## Setting the stage for discussing reliability and validity

Are diagnostic manuals **reliable** and **valid**?

The dominant manuals, the DSM-5 and the ICD-10, have become more reliable over time.

To what degree are the manuals valid? Validity is more controversial. Right now the answer is that diagnostic manuals are valid *to some extent*. Horwitz (2005) believes that validity should be valued over reliability. DSM-I and DSM-II situated a diagnosis within one's life context and were highly valid. The move to symptom-based diagnosis in the DSM-III and IV improved reliability but compromised validity. DSM-5 still focuses on reliability, but includes some attempts to increase validity, such as using severity ratings to help define an individual's experience.

Increasing reliability decreases validity and vise versa. No diagnostic system effectively balances reliability and validity. No one agrees on which is more valuable.

## A brief history of the DSM and ICD

A brief history of three diagnostic systems, the **DSM-5**, published in 2013, the **ICD-10**, published in 1992 and up for revision by 2015, and the **CCMD-3**, published in 2001, helps students understand why mental disorders are not real things. The DSM and the ICD are the most dominant of the diagnostic systems. The CCMD is a national classification system (Parker, Gladstone, & Chee, 2001). The first CCMD was published in 1979 and gave respectability to Chinese psychiatry. CCMD-1 appeared in 1981, CCMD-2 in 1984, and CCMD-3 in 2001. CCMD-2 was revised for reliability with the DSM and the ICD manuals. The CCMD-3 is similar to the DSM and the ICD but contains some disorders relevant to the Chinese, such as neurasthenia, Qi Kung disorder, and disorders due to witchcraft.

Most cultures have a way of classifying mental disorder. Sometimes a cultural group does not believe that sets of symptoms similar to western "mental illnesses" are real mental disorders. Although the DSM, the ICD, and the CCMD are examples of classification, other ways of thinking, such as the beliefs of the Baganda of Uganda discussed in chapter 4, illustrate schemas from other cultures.

Understanding the *assumptions* of diagnostic manuals helps in evaluating their reliability and validity.

DSM-IV-TR (American Psychiatric Association, 2000) included a section outlining its history, claiming that physicians have always needed to classify mental illnesses. The authors included the blunt statement, "There has been little agreement on which disorders should be included and the optimal method for their organization" (p. xxiv).

The classification of mental disorders had varied purposes and organization over the past two centuries. The number of disorders in each system changes. Sometimes the purpose was to collect statistical data while other times the purpose was to find the right help for patients.

## The first classification systems
Collecting statistics was the goal of the first U.S. classification systems, starting with the 1840 census report that had just one classification, idiocy/insanity. Seven categories were used in the 1880 census, including mania and melancholia. Even in 1917, data on mental health were still used for statistical purposes. After 1917, the American Medical Association included psychiatric disorder in its Standard Classified Nomenclature of Disease.

Responding to the needs of World War II Veterans, the U.S. Army and the Veterans Administration developed a broader classification system for mental disorders. At the same time, the World Health Organization (WHO) included mental disorders into the sixth edition of the ICD. The ICD-6 had ten psychotic disorders, nine neurotic disorders, and seven disorders of character, behavior, and intelligence. Each new edition of the DSM and the ICD was made in collaboration.

## DSM I and II
DSM-I appeared in 1952, a modification of the ICD-6. The American Psychiatric Association developed DSM-I as a way to find the right treatment for patients. DSM-I used the term *reaction* throughout the manual to mean mental disorders were a reaction to biological, social, and psychological factors. *This makes **etiology**, or causes, a primary assumption of DSM-I diagnosis.*

DSM-II was similar to DSM-I except the term *reaction* was removed. *It was a move away from diagnosing mental illness with causation.*

The first two editions were highly **valid**. Theories of causation help us understand a person's situation. *Highly* *valid diagnoses have low reliability*, making it hard for different health providers to talk about the same thing. Critics such as David Rosenhan pushed for more reliable systems. Rosenhan (1973) sent seven friends and colleagues to mental hospitals throughout the country, instructing them to complain of hearing voices. All were admitted, and then showed no other signs of mental illness. The pseudopatients stayed in the hospitals from seven to fifty-three days. Hospital personnel handed out drugs, which no one took, and treated the pseudopatients as if they were mentally ill, even though no one really had a disorder. The study shocked the psychiatric community and was one motivation to create a reliable system.

## DSM-III and IV

DSM-III appeared in 1980. Unlike the first two editions, it was organized in clusters of symptoms where the *context* of the illness was eliminated (Horwitz, 2005). A symptom-based system assumes that causation is unimportant, and that anyone having a certain number of symptoms has a disorder, thus increasing reliability. Clinicians with different theoretical orientations more easily agree on lists of symptoms.

The move away from context *increased reliability at the expense of validity*. DSM-III was neutral to causation, consisting of specific *descriptions* of disorders (American Psychiatric Association, 2000).

DSM-IV kept the symptom-based approach. However, the American Psychiatric Association task force for DSM-IV admitted that coming up with "absolute and infallible criteria" (p. xxviii) was impossible. No diagnostic manual is perfect, so tolerate uncertainty.

The DSM-IV task force considered proposals for many new diagnoses. Those added to DSM-IV were based on research, though there was no way to include everything. *The authors of DSM-IV knew there were limits to its categories.* There was no assumption that categories were discrete. In addition, a category system works best if everyone is the same and there are "clear boundaries between cases" (p. xxxi). The obvious problem in applying a categorical system is that the problems of real clients seen in clinical practice do not fit neatly into a discrete category.

Cultural considerations were new to DSM-IV, though *culture was not essential to DSM-IV diagnosis, limiting its validity.* Cultural considerations were part of an appendix and related to understanding culture-bound disorders.

## DSM-5

DSM-5 offers many changes to diagnoses, though it is overall similar to DSM-IV in that it focuses on a reliable, symptom-based system.

DSM-5 changes include the following (Grohol, 2012, Jabr, 2012).

1. Severity ratings are required for each symptom to understand an individual's diagnosis and track progress.
2. The bereavement exclusion for diagnosing depression is out, meaning people grieving the loss of a loved one can qualify for a diagnosis of depression after only a two-week time-period.
3. Some disorders are out, such as Aspergers' Syndrome. People diagnosed with Aspergers' might now qualify for Autistic Spectrum Disorder.
4. DSM-5 contains some new disorders. One is binge eating disorder, defined as lacking control over what to

eat and when, and consuming more than a normal person in the same amount of time in the same circumstances.
5. Some disorders are combined into a single diagnosis. For example, substance abuse and dependence are joined under one new disorder, substance use disorder, relevant for students studying health psychology. Internet addiction did not make it into DSM-5, but a disorder called Internet Use Gaming Disorder is identified for further research and possible inclusion later.
6. DSM-5 moves away from the Roman numeral system, motivated by the need to have an online version of the manual that can be frequently changed. In the future, look for DSM-5.1, DSM-5.2 and so on.

Critics attacked DSM-5 from its conception, including (a) medicalizing everyday life experiences, (b) inclusiveness was motivated by drug companies seeking patients, and (c) some real problems seen in clinical practice were excluded.

The National Institute of Mental Health issued a statement declaring DSM-5 was reliable, yet invalid (Insel, 2012). Insel claims DSM-5 is "At best, a dictionary, creating a set of labels and defining each" (p. 1). The NIMH's future research goal is to create a diagnostic system based on biological markers that have specific cognitive and emotional effects similar to physical illnesses. Historically, NIMH research rejected biological markers that were not directly relevant to DSM diagnostic criteria. The split opens the door for new research and perhaps a different type of diagnosis system in the future.

Note to the teacher:

> Are we **DSMizing** the world? Consider the article titled, *Are somatoform disorders changing with time?: The case of neurasthenia* (Sing & Kleinman, 2007). The article covered the increased rates of mental illness in China that mirrored pressures for the Chinese Classification of Mental Disorders (CCMD-3) to become similar to the DSM. What are the consequences of DSMizing? Might traditional cultures disappear?
>
> One consequence relates to etiologies of depression. Chapter 7 includes a section on culture and gene expression. **Gene-culture co-evolution** theory, an evolutionary explanation of behavior for Paper 1, suggests mental illness is low in traditional Asian cultures because collectivist values may lower stress and prevent genes from expressing in populations carrying higher risk factors. This is another example where the IB learning outcomes interrelate.

DSM-5 supporters claim the new manual is structured to get people the help they need. For example, the bereavement exclusion for depression was a good thing because some people were labeled grieving in the past when they were really depressed, missing out on needed treatment for long periods of time. Now psychiatrists have the option to use a depression diagnosis.

Some new research will examine DSM-5 categories while some research will follow revised NIMH goals. Expect to see heated debate and a continued evolving diagnostic system.

# Chapter 4

# Discuss cultural and ethical considerations in diagnosis

Prevalence rates are incorrect unless psychologists diagnose persons from all cultures accurately. Over and under-diagnosis are the potentially dangerous and *unethical* results of strictly applying western diagnostic criteria cross-culturally. If culture affects diagnosis and these concerns are left unaddressed, then the **validity** of diagnostic systems is compromised.

Avoid judging people from other cultures without investigating their situations with an open mind— one IB **learner profile** goal. We run the risk of **ethnocentrism** if "variation" is interpreted as deviating from a "real" standard set in a western diagnostic manual. Ethnocentric people treat their own culture as if it was the model by which all cultures should be judged.

## What is important to consider about culture and the validity of diagnosis?
Cultural psychiatry views behavior within the cultural context (Marsella & Yamada, 2007). Unfortunately, reliable diagnostic manuals do just the opposite, and they *decontextualize* mental illness. Western diagnostic manuals fail to take *situational factors* affecting the person into account, consistent with the conclusion that people have a

tendency to make dispositional **attributions** and ignore situational factors shaping behavior. Many mental illnesses stem from family and community problems.

In addition, studies investigating culture and mental illness come from western thinking, even if the studies are meant to be cross-cultural. Researchers too often have the view that mental illness in another culture is a variation of a "real" mental disorder seen in the West. Psychiatrists practicing in nonwestern countries often are required to use the western standards but find they are not really useful for behaviors in other cultural contexts.

Western diagnostic systems are *dominant* rather than *accurate*. The focus on consistent diagnoses using the DSM and ICD might overshadow local diagnostic systems.

Six situational factors contribute to mental illness across culture, particularly depression.

1. Social conditions such as "war, natural disasters, racism, poverty, cultural collapse, aging populations, urbanization, and rapid social and technological changes" (p. 811) are important.
2. Western depression may be linked to an abstract language separating people from daily experiences, emphasizing guilt, and highlighting values related to **individualism**. In contrast, people in nonwestern cultures experience depression primarily through physical symptoms that show a unity of mind and body.
3. Media messages contribute to depressive symptoms.
4. Social class is a factor. Depression and social class are negatively correlated, meaning that as social class lowers, depression rates rise.
5. Powerlessness, inequality, racism, and cultural disintegration contribute to poor mental health.

6. The **stigma** of mental illness makes many people unwilling to accept a diagnosis and treatment. Displays of western mental illness symptoms often contrasts expected cultural norms. Stigmatization and cultural disintegration are potential results.

## Classification of eating disorders: A specific example of the concern and positive changes

**Norms** about food consumption and body shape differ across cultures, so it follows that symptoms of body image and disordered eating differ (Becker, 2007).

**Etics** and **emics** are useful concepts for understanding the limitations of the DSM-IV category for anorexia. Studying the history of diagnosing eating disorders is a good example of the correct use of the concepts.

## Etics/Emics Overview

- Etics and emics are research tools that make cultures comparable.
- Etics are universal continuums and every culture falls somewhere on the continuum. Examples are marriage and all dimensions of culture, including time orientation and individualism-collectivism.
- Emics are specific cultural practices, such as a particular marriage ceremony or being future or present time oriented.
- Berry (1969) brought emics and etics to psychology from anthropology and outlined their proper use.
- Researchers begin their studies with an etic in mind, or something assumed to be universal, often something observed in the West. An intense fear of fat was a presumed etic from studying some western cases of anorexia.
- Over time, researchers see cultural behavior that may suggest an assumed etic is incorrect.
- Researchers next redefine the etic to describe all cultures and make adjustments as often as needed, ending in an etic that applies to all.
- All psychology concepts must be etics to ensure they apply to everyone. For example, is conformity an etic? It is because everyone falls on the continuum from not conforming to extreme conforming and we can compare cultures in experiments.

DSM-5 includes changes to classifying **anorexia** (AN) that can make future diagnosis more accurate, ethical, and cross-culturally relevant. A DSM-IV diagnosis of AN was not possible without an extreme fear of gaining weight or being fat that has been removed from DSM-5. The consequences of requiring a "fat phobia" resulted in many cases of over and under-diagnosis over the years. Self-starvation cases exist all over the world (Keel, 2005). *The fat phobia was not universal and made international relevance of AN impossible.* "When the fear of fat criteria is removed, AN is seen with equal frequency in Western and nonwestern cultures" (p. 23).

Correct diagnosis involves properly using **etics** and **emics**. Etic approaches apply universal diagnostic systems to everyone, usually based on western classifications. An intense fear of getting fat, the "fat phobia" was an etic seen in many western patients. Assessment tests, such as the Eating Disorders Attitude Scale (EAT-26) that try to measure the etics, are *intended* to have cross-culturally **reliability** and **validity**.

The etic approach is inadequate, though its intention is to make cross-cultural data comparable.

An emic approach starts with locally meaningful contexts for eating disordered symptoms. An emic approach is a good way to collect data, though it compromises comparability.

Next are examples of over and under-diagnosis from using limited DSM-IV definitions of AN that ignored emic expressions of disordered eating. These examples, along with the efforts of researchers such as Anne Becker, contributed to DSM-5 changes.

Persons from Hong Kong, Japan, Singapore, Malaysia, South Africa, and India can have all the other symptoms of

AN except the fat phobia (Becker, 2007). Persons from Hong Kong have been misclassified as non-cases of eating disorders based on the EAT-26 simply because they lacked a fat phobia. Black adolescents from South Africa who tested positively for disordered eating with the EAT-26 clarified in follow-up interviews that they were preoccupied with food because of poverty, hunger, and food shortages. Knowledge of a person's social context is vital.

In addition, attitudes about food consumption complicate the etic approach. During Fijian feasting, local herbal tonics are used for purging after culturally sanctioned overeating. The behavior may look like binging and purging, but traditional Fijian culture does not consider it disordered. A local Fijian diagnosis exists for **macake**, an appetite disorder that is not similar to anything in the West. Persons with macake refuse food and have poor appetites, behaviors that arouse great social concern. Macake is usually brief since persons are willing to take herbal supplements to restore their appetite. The behaviors lack meaning unless we are aware of the social context.

The DSM-5 AN category can help people from many cultures get the diagnosis when it is the correct one, which prevents over and under-diagnosis. In addition, emic expressions of body image, norms about food consumption, and local situations are respected. Instead of requiring a fat phobia, DSM-5 uses general language that requires a *continual behavior that prevents weight gain when the person is already at a very low weight.*

Becker added that even people *within* western populations were frequently misdiagnosed under the DSM-IV anorexia category because it was too limited, such as needing a "fat phobia." The most frequent eating disorder in the West under DSM-IV was "eating disorder not otherwise specified" (EDNOS).

Comparisons between DSM-IV and DSM-5 diagnoses for eating disorders show that using DSM-5 will increase correct diagnoses and lessen the number of diagnoses of "eating disorders not otherwise specified" (Keel, Brown, Holm-Denoma, & Bodell, 2011). The researchers examined U.S. university student questionnaires about disordered eating and results included the following.
1. DSM-IV showed 14% of the sample would get AN while DSM-5 showed 20% had AN.
2. DSM-IV showed 68% had an eating disorder not otherwise specified and DSM-5 showed only 8%.

## Cultural syndromes

Students may have heard the phrase "culture-bound disorders" from studying DSM-IV. DSM-5 changes the language to **cultural syndromes** because clusters of symptoms exist in some places that are not recognized outside of the culture (American Psychiatric Association, 2013). DSM-5 does not contain similar symptom clusters and health providers must use caution before applying DSM categories to people showing these syndromes. Does the category really fit? The Cultural Formulation Interview (CFI), outlined in chapter 1, is one way to clarify the situation.

Examples of cultural syndromes in DSM-5 include the following that are similar but not exactly the same as depression.
1. **Susto**, a Hispanic fright illness
2. **Shenjing Shuairu**, a disorder seen in China that focuses on physical complaints

3. **Nervios**, a common way for Latinos to describe general stressful events
4. **Kufungisisa**, or "thinking too much" in the Shona of Zimbabwe

## To what extent are Uganda's Baganda depressed in a western sense?

Should Ugandan's Baganda make use of the western depression diagnosis? One right answer does not exist, but class discussion about cultural and ethical considerations in diagnosis, prevalence rates, causes, and treatments of depression arises from considering the question.

Individual and focus group interviews using case vignettes explore local perceptions of depressive symptoms in the Baganda of Uganda (Okello & Ekblad, 2006). Vignettes are short stories.

Depressive symptoms in Uganda are often expressed and referred to as an **"illness of thought"** rather than an emotional illness. Illnesses of thoughts do not require medicine because no medicine exists for thinking. Medical help is required only in cases of constant or recurring illness.

The Bagandan view shows the complexities of diagnosis. If a local population does not recognize a group of symptoms as depression, it is unlikely to be received as a diagnosis. The Bagandans have their own way of thinking about mental illness that matches cultural expectations.

The prevalence of depressive symptoms in Uganda is high, between 10-25%, largely because of its violent history and the large number of HIV/AIDS cases. Although observations made in Ugandan psychiatric clinics suggest depression is common, the people of Uganda rarely recognize it as such. About 70 to 90% of mental health problems in Uganda never reach mental health services.

Note to the teacher:

> Your class can decide the extent to which the Bagandan symptoms should be considered "depressed" and treated as such, or if the symptoms are a cultural syndrome that should be treated by local healers when possible.

The interviews took place in Bajjo, a small semi-rural district close to the capital. Next is some background on the Baganda necessary to interpret the case vignettes.

The clan system dominates the way Bagandans think about others. No one is thought about without reference to patrilineal descent. Clan members are viewed as extended family, even if blood ties are distant. The clan is a hierarchy with the clan leader at the top. All clans have a primary and secondary totem, a symbol for the clan often taking the form of an animal or plant. Everyone introduces themselves to others in the context of the clan.

The Baganda believe in superhuman spirits where a person's spirit remains after death. Many other African cultures share this belief. Several types of spirits are important to the Baganda. One is *mizimu*, ghosts of the dead. These spirits seek people the dead person holds a grudge against. *Misambwa* are objects the mizimu has entered. *Balubaale* are spirits that have the talents of outstanding men. All three spirits are called *byekika*, or "the clan things." Spirits are believed to influence health and are divided into two general groups, the family or community spirits that aid in health unless they are upset, and alien or evil spirits causing trouble.

The Baganda connect illnesses with body parts. For example, a cough is labeled "chest." Depressive symptoms stem from thoughts or the heart, so depression is connected to either, such as "illness of thoughts." Illnesses are further broken down into ones treated by traditional healers or folk remedies and ones treated by western doctors.

Five individual participants responded to the vignettes, including three traditional healers and one faith healer. Other participants took part in four different focus groups of six each representing different societal layers. The focus groups were secondary school girls, village women, village men, and primary school teachers. Variables influencing the perception of individuals in each focus group, such as age and educational level, were controlled.

DSM-IV was used to create the vignettes. A series of stories illustrated different experiences with depression and participants considered if they knew anyone fitting the descriptions.

The researchers used five vignettes for the study. Two examples are next.

One case was a twenty-eight year-old person with major depression symptoms without psychotic features. The symptoms included unhappiness, a lack of enjoyment of usual activities, a closed mind, feelings of emptiness, sleeping difficulties, a change in eating habits, no energy, thoughts that life was no longer worth living, wandering thoughts, and thoughts of death and suicide.

All thirty participants connected the vignette with their own experience or someone they knew. Almost everyone described the symptoms as "too many worrisome thoughts." Participants decided the thoughts were under the person's control and recommended avoiding the thoughts. Few considered the person "mad." While the "illnesses of thought" were identified as a mental illness, most considered treatments by traditional healers more appropriate than western medicine. Traditional healers viewed the symptoms as "mild madness" resulting from witchcraft. Both the lay participants and traditional healers supported local customs where traditional healers treated all illnesses resulting from community or cultural causes.

Another case was a thirty-eight-year old man or woman with recurring dysthymia, meaning persistent mild depression, for four years. The person felt uncomfortable, complained of bodily aches and pains, and thought a neighbor was bewitching him or her. This person had received treatment from a local mental health clinic without success, and from a local healer. The focus group said the symptoms were the result of a genes, HIV, and/or witchcraft. The symptoms were a combination of biomedical and local beliefs. The men's focus group added that the symptoms were a recent problem and had no formal name in their language, though they believed it was the result of everyday life conditions, such as lacking money.

Four categories of mental illness causation emerged from the interviews.
1. The first was psychological factors that came from thinking too much about things such as relationship problems.
2. The second was socioeconomic factors such as job loss.
3. The third was spiritual factors such as witchcraft and angry ancestral gods.

4. The fourth was biological or physical factors, such as genes or constant physical illness, which was reserved for cases with recurring symptoms. Eighty percent of the participants thought depressive symptoms came from social stress and viewed the symptoms as "illness of thoughts" best treated by spiritual healers.

Only recurring symptoms were linked to genetics or constant illness requiring western medical care. Local healers treated the cases, even if people also benefited from western biomedicine.

Seeking help from family, friends, clan elders, religious leaders and traditional healers was stressed by all participants. Traditional healers were recommended when the illness was caused by witchcraft, angry ancestral gods, or had an unknown cause. One focus group member said the lack of western mental health services was a reason western medicine was not used.

The researchers highlighted some limitations of using focus groups. **Informants** helped the researchers gain access to study participants, and local authorities could have biased the study by recommending particular people as informants. The use of specifically designed vignettes in the individual interviews may have limited the discussion to just those situations.

## Eclectic treatments: Combining local healers with western treatments to satisfy needs of local communities

If it is important to consider culture and ethics in diagnosis, it makes sense to extend the argument all the way to the end. Which treatments go with a culturally relevant diagnosis that might be ignored without careful attention to cultural practices?

Local healers offer important mental health treatments (Abbo, Ekblad, Waako, Okello, & Musisi, 2009). The aim of the study was to examine the prevalence and severity of the disorders treated by local healers in two Uganda communities. Interviews with four hundred participants showed that 60.2 % had a current mental illness and 16.3 % had a mental illness sometime over their life span. Many had moderate or severe symptoms and went to the shrine where traditional healers offered treatment. Most people said they did not ask for help unless symptoms were severe and then first went to traditional headers. Some traditional healers even specialize in treating psychotic cases.

The authors concluded that *western attitudes condemning traditional healing were unproductive.* Western mental health workers should find ways to work with traditional healers to respect cultural values and provide the highest quality of care in a setting where resources to fund costly medical care are limited.

Other research confirms that local traditional healers offer beneficial treatments, even for psychotic disorders such as severe depression (Abbo, Okello, Muisi, Waako, & Ekblad, 2012). The researchers found that 80% of psychotic patients combined traditional healing and biomedical medicine successfully and recovered after three months.

Note to the teacher:

> Combining local traditional healers and western biomedical medicine is an example of **eclectic**, or combination treatments. Although combining traditional healing in Uganda with western drugs is a new field, it is an example of the dangers and possible unethical treatment of people from other cultures if not considered. The reviewed research offers culturally relevant and ethical ways to lessen mental illness.
>
> Abbo's research is an example of what Patel recommended in the book's introduction to empower local communities.

# Chapter 5

# Describe symptoms and prevalence of Major Depression: the example for affective disorders

"Major depressive disorder, also called major depression, is characterized by a combination of symptoms that interfere with a person's ability to work, sleep, study, eat, and enjoy once-pleasurable activities. Major depression is disabling and prevents a person from functioning normally. An episode of major depression may occur only once in a person's lifetime, but more often, it recurs throughout a person's life" (NIMH, 2008, p. 1).

Let's compare **DSM-5** and **CCMD-3** symptoms and prevalence rates for major depression.

## DSM-5 diagnosis for major depression, prevalence reports, and culture related diagnostic issues

To receive a diagnosis of major depressive disorder, five symptoms from the list must occur during the same two-week period (American Psychiatric Association, 2013). The symptoms must be very different from a person's normal

regular behavior. *One of the symptoms must be depressed mood or loss of interest or pleasure.*
1. Self-reports or information from others show the person has depressed mood most of the day each day.
2. Self-reports or information from others show the person has a significantly lowered interest and pleasure in activities all day almost every day.
3. The person experiences changes in appetite and/or weight. This means a 5% weight gain or loss when not dieting occurs or one's appetite increases or decreases almost every day.
4. Almost every day, the person suffers from insomnia or hypersomnia (extreme sleepiness).
5. Reports from others show the person is physically too active or not active enough.
6. The person is tired or has low energy almost every day.
7. The person feels worthless or shows too much or inappropriate guilt almost every day.
8. The person cannot concentrate or is indecisive almost every day.
9. The person has frequent thoughts of dying that are not just fears of dying. The person has thoughts of suicide without a plan, has plans for suicide, or has attempted suicide.

Severity ratings are included for each person, including mild, moderate, severe, and with psychotic features. Severity ratings might help people get the best treatment and track treatment effectiveness.

**Prevalence** rates in the U.S., over a twelve-month period, is about 7%. Rates vary by age and gender. Female depression rates are up to three times higher than males and the differences show starting in adolescence. People aged eighteen to twenty-nine have depression rates three times higher than people over sixty.

Prevalence rates across **culture** vary greatly, with some cultures showing seven times the amount of depression. Data suggests great variation in the number of people with depressive symptoms, but the American Psychiatric Association warns not to assume that specific cultural practices lead to particular symptoms. In addition, the American Psychiatric Association believes many depression cases go unrecognized in primary care settings in most countries and can present as somatic complaints, meaning bodily symptoms.

Note to the teacher:

> The class might discuss the extent to which more cases of depression should be diagnosed. Watch taking extreme positions. Consider the issues—on one hand the American Psychiatric Association believes that depression goes unrecognized in many countries but on the other hand some cultures, such as the Baganda of Uganda, discussed in chapter 4, have a cultural interpretation of depressive symptoms. A Chinese view of depressive symptoms follows under the next heading. Make sure to read the Kleinman article, as discussed in chapter 2.

CCMD-3 diagnosis for depressive episode

The CCMD-3 (Chinese Society of Psychiatry, 2003) contains a disorder called "depressive episode" similar to DSM-5 major depressive disorder but with some differences reflecting its use in Chinese culture. To receive this diagnosis, a person must have a depressed mood different from life circumstances. The depressed mood must include four of the symptoms in the list below. These symptoms refer to a single episode of depression. Separate diagnoses are used for recurrent depression and mild depression. A diagnosis of recurrent depression requires that any type of depression must occur within the past two months. Mild depression is the same as depressive episode but the impairment in social behavior is mild.

1. The person has a loss of interest in or loss of enjoyment.
2. The person has low energy or fatigue.
3. The person is either physically agitated or shows little motor activity.
4. The person has low self-esteem, feels worthless, is self-blaming, or is preoccupied with guilt.
5. The person is unable to focus their thinking.
6. The person has attempted some kind of self-harm or suicide or has thoughts of doing either.
7. The person has insomnia, wakes too early in the morning, or has hypersomnia.
8. The person has little appetite or obvious weight loss.
9. The person has a decreased libido.

The CCMD-3 includes a separate diagnosis for **Neurasthenia**. Chinese persons often express depressive symptoms as somatic complaints. Neurasthenia is then a more appropriate diagnosis, though it is not used as widely as it once was. Neurasthenia is classified in the group of disorders called Hysteria, stress related disorders, Neurosis.

Neurasthenia is listed as a *neurosis*. The main symptoms are mental and physical weaknesses. The person is easily excited and fatigued, and is tense, annoyed, or irritated. The person has sleep problems and muscle tension or pain. These symptoms are not part of another disorder and continue over several months. The person may have high stress levels and may suddenly start to have headaches and difficulty sleeping.

Neurasthenia includes the following symptoms.
1. The person meets the criteria for neurosis. Neurosis is classified as a stress related disorder in the CCMD-3, which also includes phobias, panic attacks, and obsessive behavior.
2. The person has mental and physical weakness, such as a lack of vigor, poor concentration and memory, and physical fatigue that are recovered by rest, along with two of the following.
    a. The person has emotional difficulties, such as tenseness, anxiety and depression that are not the prominent symptoms, irritability and difficulty in coping with daily life.
    b. The person is easily excited, such as difficulty concentrating on one thing at a time.
    c. The person has muscle aches and pains or dizziness.
    d. The person has problems sleeping, such as insomnia.

e. The person has other psychological or physical problems, such as rapid heartbeat or tinnitus, meaning ringing or roaring noises in the ears.

## Prevalence of depression in China

The CCMD-3 does not contain prevalence rates. Exact prevalence rates probably vary a great deal by region in China.

Cultural values affect the expression and diagnosis of mental illness. Understanding symptoms and prevalence rates of depression in China requires a history lesson about mental health in China.

Note to the teacher:

> The expression of "depressive symptoms" is changing in China along with the expansion of a global community, and particularly the influence of the DSM. Consequences are great for traditional cultural values, which might even influence the etiology of mental illnesses. Cross-reference this section with the discussion of culture-gene coevolution and depression in chapter 7. Cultural and ethical considerations in diagnosis from chapter 4 are closely related. The following discussion helps students develop a sense of **internationalism**, the IB mission.

The Chinese are the world's largest ethnic group, representing approximately 22% of the world's population (Parker, Gladstone, & Chee, 2001). Do not assume that everyone in China thinks about mental health the same way. *Many factors make understanding the symptoms and prevalence rates complex.* About fifty-five ethnic groups live in China and the rapid changes occurring since the end of Mao's regime have affected the *layers* of society differently. Some parts of China have adopted western psychiatric views, some combine western and traditional Chinese views, and others have kept their beliefs exclusive to Traditional Chinese Medicine.

Depression was rarely diagnosed in China in the 1980s. In 1993, only sixteen of 19,223 persons met the criteria for an **affective disorder**, much higher than the 1982 rate. The lifetime prevalence rate for affective disorder was .08% in 1993, several hundred times lower than the U.S. rate.

Even studies on the prevalence from Taiwan, a more industrialized nation, between 1982 and 1986, show the prevalence of depression is low.

Reasons for the low rate include a) an actual low rate, b) low reporting because of social **stigma**, or c) the presence of other disorders similar to depression but more culturally valid for the Chinese.

Chinese psychiatrists have not historically diagnosed depression as often as they have other disorders. For example, in Hunan province, only 1% of the patients were diagnosed with depression while 30% received the diagnosis for neurasthenia. Adding to the complexities is the typical attitude toward doctors. For example, people are more likely to consult a Traditional Chinese Medical (TCM) doctor for problems they consider "illnesses" and a western type doctor for problems they categorize as "diseases." *Chinese persons do not generally consider emotional upset a disease.*

Does a true western depression exist in China? It has a CCMD-3 category, but the relevance of depressive symptoms is embedded in the history of how the Chinese think about mental illness. *The Chinese may deemphasize depressive symptoms as defined by western standards, but in turn, depression may be over emphasized and pathologized in the West.*

TCM was the primary care for mental health problems in China until the beginning of the 1900s (Chinese Society of Psychiatry, 2005). TCM makes no distinction between mental and physical health. All mental and physical health problems are Chi, or energy, imbalances treated with acupuncture, herbs, and lifestyle changes.

In the early 1900s, new ideas came to China and neurasthenia was one of those new ideas (Parker, et al., 2001). Neurasthenia was a condition where a person experiences **somatic**, or bodily, symptoms. In China, neurasthenia was called **shenjing shuairuo**, meaning neurological weakness. Shenjing shuairuo was common. Approximately 80% of psychiatric patients in China received the diagnosis of neurasthenia during the 1980s. People without much experience and knowledge of western mental disorders experience distress physically, symptoms less **stigmatizing**.

Another factor is the various translations of the word depression, which can mean "repress," "gloomy," or "disorder," all of which are unpopular with the Chinese.

Last, political history influenced attitudes toward depression. Mao thought psychology was "ninety percent useless" and mental illnesses were incorrect political thinking. Political policy amplified the social stigma of mental illness, which made *neurasthenia a socially acceptable diagnosis.* Many words in the Chinese language describe emotions, so a language problem does not explain behavior. Somatic symptoms are *a cultural preference, a "display rule," that dictates what the Chinese report to doctors*. The Chinese speak in metaphors relating to their emotions that are physical in nature.

In the 1980s, China opened to western influence, which included western psychiatric practice. By the time the DSM-III appeared, Chinese psychiatrists thought most neurasthenia cases could be re-diagnosed as depression. Chinese doctors realized the diagnosis of depression gave them a new treatment option, antidepressant drugs. There were no antineurasthenia drugs.

Although neurasthenia became less popular with modern Chinese psychiatrists, it was still preferred by the typical person as a diagnosis throughout the 1990s.

Rates of depression in China continued to increase and the diagnosis of neurasthenia continued to decrease over a fairly short time span, so fast that social factors must be the reason for the changes (Lee & Kleinman, 2007). Lee and Kleinman claim that **DSMizing** the world may or may not bring the best treatments to local communities. DSMizing is discussed in the next "note to the teacher" text-box.

Does a low rate of depression also occur in Chinese populations outside of China? Studies show that the rates are still lower in westernized Chinese populations (Parker, et al., 2001).

Are the Chinese just more **resilient** to depression? Sociocultural factors seem to promote resilience in the Chinese, such as accepting hardship and valuing interdependence with family.

Note to the teacher:

The IB mission revolves around developing **internationalism** in students. What is the impact of western psychiatric global influence on traditional culture? What are potential gains and losses? Sing and Kleinman (2007) warn that the global **DSMization** of psychiatry comes with consequences. To what extent is exporting western diagnosis ethical? Does DSMizing help people get more effective treatments?

The Sing and Kleinman article is recommended for teachers.

# Chapter 6

# Describe symptoms and prevalence of Anorexia Nervosa (AN): the example for eating disorders

Eating disorders involve a "persistent disturbance of eating or eating related behavior that results in the altered consumption or absorption of food and that significantly impairs physical health or psychological functioning" (American Psychiatric Association, 2013, p. 329).

DSM-5 *makes fundamental changes to diagnosing* **anorexia nervosa** (AN) that include new language allowing real cases of AN to be detected and cross-cultural friendliness. For example, DSM-5 drops the requirement of an intense fear of fat, the "fat phobia." The ICD-10 still contains a requirement for the intense fear of getting fat, which may disappear in its new edition. A fear of getting fat has always been *possible but not required* for a CCMD-3 diagnosis. Cultural differences in attitudes about weight account for the CCMD-3 language about fears of fat.

Anorexia nervosa as a medical term first appeared in 1874 as the way William Gull described the symptoms of four girls who deliberately lost weight (Keel, 2005). So eating disorders existed before modern times. Historically,

AN was not linked to a fear of fat. Instead, AN was self-starvation related to moral beliefs and attention seeking. The DSM-IV diagnosis in for AN changed the historical meaning of AN to include an assumed **etic** based on modern, perhaps western, cultural influences concerning weight and body shape. Research showing **emic** expressions of disordered eating helped create a better universal etic for AN in DSM-5.

In addition, DSM-5 removes the requirement for amenorrhea, or loss of the menstrual cycle, because many girls do not lose it and the requirement is irrelevant for males.

While AN exists historically, there has been a modest increase in its diagnosis over time.

Anne Becker was on the DSM-5 committee for feeding and eating disorders, and her work is referenced in chapter 4 about cultural and ethical considerations in diagnosis and chapter 8 about etiologies of AN.

## DSM-5 diagnosis for anorexia nervosa (AN)

The DSM-5 (American Psychiatric Association, 2013) categorizes AN under the heading of feeding and eating disorders. Eating disorders include AN, bulimia nervosa (BN), and a new category for binge eating disorder (BED).

The DSM-5 lists the symptoms of AN as follows.
1. The person restricts energy intake in a way that differs significantly from requirements. The person has a significantly low body weight relative to what is normal or expected for their age and developmental level.
2. The person has extreme fear of gaining weight or being fat, **or** has a persistent behavior that prevents

weight gain, even though he or she is already at a significantly low weight.
3. The person denies that his or her weight loss or lack of weight gain is a serious problem, has self-evaluations showing an undue influence of body shape and weight, or persistently denies the seriousness of their low weight.

Severity ratings are mild, moderate, severe, and extreme.

DSM-5 lists two types of AN, restricting type and binge-eating/purging type. Restricting types engage in extreme fasting, dieting or exercising. Binge-eating/purging means large amounts of food are consumed and are followed by self-induced vomiting or the use of laxatives, diuretics, or enemas.

**Prevalence** of AN over a twelve-month time-period is 0.4% for females. Male prevalence rates are hard to know. Males show AN differently; this is discussed in chapter 11 about cultural and gender.

AN usually starts in adolescence or early adulthood and stressful events often proceed it. The time someone has AN and the level of recovery varies. Some fully recover after one episode of AN, some have problems with fluctuating weight and then relapse, and some people have constant problems and even die from AN. Sometimes persons with AN are hospitalized in an attempt to stabilize weight. About 5% eventually die of AN.

AN prevalence rates may vary greatly across **culture** and researchers know the most about prevalence in industrialized nations such as the U.S., European countries, Australia, and Japan. Sometime prevalence rates are hard to know in lower socioeconomic countries. Concerns about weight vary cross-culturally. Some ethnic groups living in high socioeconomic nations, such as Latinos in the U.S., do not seek help as often as Caucasian groups, so exact prevalence rates are hard to know. See chapter 9 about cultural and gender variations in prevalence for more on the topic.

## CCMD-3 diagnosis for anorexia nervosa (AN)

Eating disorders are classified as part of a group of disorders called "physiological disorders related to psychological disorders" in the CCMD-3 (Chinese Society of Psychiatry, 2003). Eating disorders include AN, bulimia nervosa, and disordered vomiting. AN is described as an adolescent female disorder where they deliberately eat less and weigh less than is considered normal. Patients sometimes worry about being fat even when they are already underweight and if a doctor tells them they are not fat. AN patients suffer from the consequences of poor nutrition as well as metabolism and hormone imbalances.

The symptoms include the following.

1. A person shows a large amount of weight loss of at least 15% below the expected weight.
2. A person deliberately loses weight and has at least one of the following.
    A. The person avoids fatty foods.
    B. The person uses self-induced vomiting to purge food.
    C. The person exercises in the extreme.
    D. The person uses drugs to lessen appetite and/or diuretics.
3. The person typically has a fear of getting fat, *but a fear is not required for a diagnosis.*

4. The person's endocrine system is out of balance. The imbalance can take numerous forms, such as amenorrhea, heightened levels of growth hormone, and high cortisol levels.
5. The symptoms have lasted for at least three months.

## Prevalence rates of AN in nonwestern countries

Prevalence rates of AN are not included in the CCMD-3.

Prevalence rates of AN in some Chinese samples are included in the following survey study about prevalence of eating disorders in nonwestern countries (Makino, Tsuboi, & Dennerstein, 2004). Generally, AN is *increasing* in nonwestern countries.

Prevalence rates of AN in nonwestern countries include the following.

1. In 1989 there were few cases of AN recorded in Hong Kong.
2. By 1991 there was a small rise of reported AN cases in Hong Kong to .46%
3. In 1996, 6.5% of females in Hong Kong showed disordered eating.
4. In 1998, 8.5% of both male and female adults in Korea showed disordered eating.
5. In 1999, 5.4% of both male and female Japanese high school students showed disordered eating attitudes.
6. In 2000, 4.1% of Japanese males and females showed disordered eating.
7. By 2003, disordered eating rates increased to 11.2% in Japanese samples.

8. In 1982, seven cases of AN were reported in Chinese females living in Singapore.
9. By 1997, fifty cases of AN were reported in Chinese females living in Singapore.

The prevalence of AN in China may be correlated with westernization. AN prevalence increased in many Asian countries throughout the 1990s, including Japan, Hong Kong, Taiwan, and the Republic of Korea (Lee, 2000). When Asian governments loosened restrictions on advertising, rates of AN rose in Asian countries such as China, India, and the Philippines. Cases of self-starvation existed in China before westernization, so AN was never exclusive to the West. However, many cases of AN in nonwestern culture involve females with exposure to western culture.

Keel (2005) reports the lifetime prevalence rate for AN as 0.9% for Iranian schoolgirls. Between 0.05% and 0.16% of mental health cases in Malaysia and 0.19% of cases in Egypt are related to AN.

# Chapter 7

# Analyze etiologies of two mental disorders: Major Depression

## A frame of reference for considering depression

A statement from the New England Journal of Medicine is a good place to start. "**Depression** is a heterogeneous disorder with a highly variable course, an inconsistent response to treatment, and no established mechanism" (Belmaker & Agam, 2008, p. 55). It means people diagnosed with depression have an assortment of symptoms, have different experiences with it, respond differently to treatments, and there is no agreement among psychologists about the causes.

No simple answers exist in the real world. Discard any preexisting ideas that depression is a specific thing. Any text identifying "causes" in such a way as to make them appear distinct and easy to verify is oversimplified and misleading. *Tolerating uncertainty is the best strategy.*

So how should we think about depression? **Stress** and **cultural schema** are useful unifying principles.

Stress is a primary factor *contributing* to depression and all other mental disorders. "Contributing" factors is a more realistic framework than "causes."

Although depressive symptoms are universal and rates are increasing, cultural schemas influence how depression is experienced and treated. "The way in which depression is confronted, discussed, and managed varies among social worlds, and cultural meanings and practices shape its course" (Kleinman, 2004, p.1).

The list of factors contributing to depression is long.

Note to the teacher:

> The IB syllabus directs students to analyze biological, cognitive, and/or sociocultural etiologies for two mental disorders. This chapter covers all three levels of analysis for depression and the next chapter covers all three levels of analysis for anorexia. Teachers have the choice of picking one or two levels of analysis for each disorder or using them all so students have choices on the exam. The biological etiologies are particularly useful for three different Paper 1 learning outcomes.

The following is a list of international factors that increase one's risk of depression, broken down into biological, cognitive, and sociocultural factors.

### Biological level of analysis:
Genes, such as 5-HTT, the serotonin transporter gene
Sleep patterns, for example, EEGs show that some depressed persons go into REM sleep rapidly, just after 60 minutes, about 20 minutes earlier than non-depressed persons

Hormone imbalances
Neurotransmitter imbalances
Asymmetry of brain hemispheres, such as EEGs showing that some depressed persons have lower activity in the left prefrontal region
Qi (or Chi, energy) imbalance
Poor diet
Lack of proper exercise
Constant illness or the presence of another mental disorder, for example, AN is associated with depression, heart disease is associated with depression
Techno-Brain Burnout
Under-stimulation of the effort reward system

**Cognitive level of analysis:**
Cognitive schemas
Negative attribution style

**Sociocultural level of analysis:**
Low self-efficacy
Marital problems
Expected female roles
The view of the self that is influenced by cultural factors
Parental maltreatment
Neighborhood factors
Poverty
Discrimination and prejudice
War
Social class
Grieving a loss
Aging populations
Natural disasters
Increased urbanization

Media messages
Lack of social support
Witchcraft
Spirits and other culturally based community causes

A *risk model* is the best way to study factors contributing to depression and is important for using the bidirectional model introduced in chapter 1.
If a person has none of the factors, then the risk of depression is low. If a person has the two short alleles of 5-HTT, the risk increases. If the person also has stressful life events, such as parent maltreatment, the risk increases a little more. If the person also lives in poverty, the risk further increases. Add low-self efficacy or a negative cognitive style and the risk increases even more. Many possible combinations exist.

No one has all the risk factors, but you see how it works. Analyzing etiologies of depression is complex because so many factors contribute to the total picture. One factor is not enough for someone to become depressed. In addition, culture mediates all factors. *Any answer to exam questions asking for one etiology of mental disorder should include a discussion of how the selected factor interacts with other factors as shown on the bidirectional model.* All mental disorders have the same framework.

It's impossible to know the exact cause of someone's depression.

The "causation" pattern is *bidirectional*. Sometimes students incorrectly think that neurotransmitter imbalances cause depression, trying to simplify the answer. Scientists are not even sure that serotonin is the main neurotransmitter responsible for depression (Lambert, 2008, Sapolsky, 2004). Be aware that many things contribute to neurotransmitter imbalance, such as genes, low self-efficacy, poor diet, or even being depressed. The argument is circular. Factors such as hormone imbalance and sleep disturbance work the same way. *This is why treatments are not always linked to cause.*

"Causation" in humans is primarily known through *correlation* studies. Strict "causation" cannot be inferred from correlation studies. While animal experiments add to our understanding of causation, animal lives are not exactly the same as human lives.

Note to the teacher:

> I start the depression unit with the film "Deeply Depressed," available from the Films for the Humanities and Sciences. The film distinguishes ordinary sadness and clinical depression and discusses the serotonin transporter gene. While the film has a western perspective, it is a good place to start because students need help distinguishing ordinary sadness from depression.

The discussion of etiologies includes genes for the biological level of analysis, depressive schemas for the cognitive level of analysis, and techno-brain burnout/ Internet overuse for the sociocultural level of analysis.

# Biological level of analysis: Background ideas for understanding genes and depression

When studying biological factors related to depression, it is important to remember that genes affect behavior but do not work alone.

People commonly blame their personality, depression, or health problems on genes. Popular media and outdated scientific theory are responsible for creating the widely held public belief that genes directly cause behavior. *We must become better consumers of media and ask good questions about scientific research.* Genes are not a direct cause of most complex human behavior. The old phrase "nature versus nurture" deserves a proper burial. Modern psychologists study the interplay between nature *and* nurture. Studying genes and depression provides a model for educating the public about the "falsehood of genetic (and environmental) determinism" (Caspi, Hariri, Holmes, Uher, & Moffitt, 2010, p.11).

Knowing that genes do not directly determine complex behavior inspires hope that we can make effective life changes and helps us understand that life events shape behavior (Peele & DeGrandpre, 1995). "Americans are increasingly likely to attribute their own—and other's—behavior to innate biological causes" (p.1). The article is aptly titled "My genes made me do it." Demands for clear causes of behavior rest on incorrect assumptions about the ways genes affect behavior. "The quest for genetic explanations of why we do what we do more accurately reflects the desire for hard certainties about frightening societal problems than the true complexities of human affairs" (p.1).

Then how do we answer the question, *to what extent do genes influence behavior?* The answer is a little tricky.

Genes are the building blocks of behavior and *contribute* to complex behavior rather than determine it. It maybe helpful to know that *genes cannot affect behavior unless they are expressed.*

The human genome contains about 25,000 genes, far fewer than most would guess. Scientists have identified several million **polymorphisms**, or variations of genes, which are probably responsible for physical and mental health problems. Polymorphisms interact with the environment and other genes to affect behavior. It takes years to study just one polymorphism, so have some awe for the process. Knowledge is steadily progressing and the goals are to prevent mental and physical illness by making people more resilient to environmental stressors and develop effective treatments. People with specific polymorphisms can be matched to prevention programs or even particular drug treatments.

Genes affect behavior through numerous pathways, studied with different methods.

Molecular genetic research methods examine how particular polymorphisms affect behavior and the future of genetic research lies with it (Caspi & Moffitt, 2006). The example studies in this book are molecular genetic studies. Molecular genetic research is different from twin and adoption research many students study that do not tell us much about particular genes. Instead, twin and adoption studies just tell us if there is *a* genetic contribution. Modern scientists want to identify specific polymorphisms so they can, for example, match treatments to polymorphisms.

**Gene X environment correlation** (GxE, interpreted as gene-environment correlation) is one molecular genetics research method used to investigate one pathway by which genes affect behavior. GxE correlations show how genes express differently in different environments. People exposed to similar environments have different responses, so genes are important and scientists can show how they interact with environmental factors and affect behavior (Caspi, et al., 2010).

## Biological level of analysis: Human genetic studies about 5-HTT and depression:

One specific gene, 5-HTT, the **serotonin transporter gene**, is prominent in research about genetic risks for **depression**. It contrasts anorexia research, the other example of mental disorder, where no gene stands out in the crowd. Avshalom Caspi's work on depression was pivotal and now used a model for studying other polymorphisms and behavior.

A polymorphism of 5-HTT *heightens one's reactivity to stress, and reactivity to stress is correlated with higher rates of depression* (Caspi, et al., 2003). The gene alone is not a reliable predictor of depression, so it must be studied as it unfolds in the environment.

Caspi's team investigated the correlation between genetic type, having one short and one long allele (s/l heterozygotes), two short alleles (s/s homozygotes) or two long alleles (l/l homozygotes) of 5-HTT, with responses on questionnaires about stressful life events and questionnaires diagnosing depression.

Everyone experiences stressors. Why do some people respond with depression? Let's use the **risk model**. Persons with large amounts of life stress have an increased risk for depression. As the number of stressful events increase, the risk increases. For people with two short alleles, the risk is even greater. The risk for depression goes down if a person has two long alleles, even in the presence of stress.

Possessing two long alleles is correlated with **resilience** to depression.

Genetic vulnerability for reacting to stress is related to a polymorphism in the promoter region of 5-HTT (Caspi, et al., 2003) Promoters are near the genes they regulate and assist in gene transcription, part of the process of gene expression, helping ensure that normal amounts of serotonin get to the brain. People with the s allele have transcriptional inefficiency, meaning that proper amounts of serotonin do not reach the brain. The serotonin transporter system is important because low levels of the neurotransmitter **serotonin** are correlated to depression, one effect of **neurotransmission** on behavior.

5-HTT is *not a direct cause* of depression, but moderates stress reactivity, and stress reactivity is correlated with higher rates of depression. Caspi's team built their study from examining previous animal and human research.

Caspi et al., (2003) used a sample of 847 Caucasians from a New Zealand database, a random sample of New Zealanders, all twenty-six years old. Participants were placed into one of three groups based on possessing one short and one long allele, two short alleles, or two long alleles.

Participants filled out a life history survey, consisting of questions about life events such as employment, health, and relationships. No difference was found in the amount of stressors experienced by participants in the three groups.

The researchers measured depression using the Diagnostic Interview Schedule. Major depression was defined as meeting DSM-IV requirements. Seventeen percent of all participants qualified for a major depression diagnosis.

Data were analyzed with correlations between depression symptoms, genotype, stressful events, and their interactions. Participants with the ss alleles had a greater risk of depression after four or more stressful events over a period of five years. Participants with the ll alleles and the same number of stressful events had a much lower risk. Reports of low stress environments predicted lower rates of depression regardless of genotype.

Correlations do not show cause and effect, but the study is part of a larger body of research about stress, genes, and depression. Approximately forty independently run studies show that the s allele "moderates the influence of stress on depression" (Caspi, et al., 2010, p. 510), so the conclusion is strong. Some studies did not replicate the findings, but several researchers have identified them as having poor study designs.

In conclusion, the gene 5-HTT affects depression greatly, but only as it interacts with stressful environments.

## Biological level of analysis: Animal genetic studies about 5-HTT and depression

Rhesus monkeys have the same 5-HTT polymorphisms as humans (Caspi, et al., 2010). Experiments using monkeys support the conclusions of human studies and often use the procedure where some baby Rhesus monkeys are taken from their mothers and raised with peers and some stay with their mothers. Clear patterns of behavior emerged. Monkeys with the l allele of 5-HTT protested their situation less. In addition, they showed effective coping skills appropriate for monkeys. Monkeys with the s allele showed more anxiety. Monkeys with the s allele also showed decreased amounts of serotonin in their spinal fluid as compared to monkeys with the short allele raised under normal living conditions in related research (Caspi, et al., 2003).

Is it ethical to place baby monkeys under stress in experiments? The American Psychological Association has rules about using animals in research stating the benefits of the research must outweigh the risk to the animal, meaning there must be a good reason for running the study. In addition, animals must be treated humanely, kept as free of pain as possible, and receive medical care. Discuss the use of animals in research with your class.

Note to the teacher:

> Research on 5-HTT in humans and animals can be used for the Paper 1 learning outcome about genetic influences on behavior. The human research can be used for the learning outcome about neurotransmission. The learning outcome about neurotransmission is specific to humans, so do not include the monkey experiment. Ethics of genetic research is also part of Paper 1.

## Biological level of analysis: The dimensions of culture and gene expression

Etiologies of depression are best understood with knowledge about the sociocultural context in which genes express. The bidirectional model is a topdown model where culture is an umbrella over cognition and biology, greatly affecting both systems.

Cultural values interact with genes and we should study the relationship for future prevention and effective treatment. **Gene-culture coevolution** has recently emerged as a theory explaining human behavior as interactions between "two complementary evolution processes, cultural and genetic evolution" (Chiao & Blizinsky, 2010, p. 529). Cultural values "are adaptive and they evolve and influence the social and physical environments under which genetic selection operates" (p. 529).

Culture affects everyone's self-construal, or the way we view the self. The **dimensions of culture** are **etics**, or universal sets of continuums reflecting the values of a group that guide self-construal. Everyone falls somewhere on the continuum. **Individualism-collectivism** is one dimension of culture studied with gene expression. Groups high on individualism value independence and self-expression. Groups high on collectivism value conformity and relationship harmony.

Genes also affect behavior, with the serotonin transporter gene and depression as one example. East Asia has greater concentrations of the risk alleles, and 70-80% carry at least one short allele of 5-HTT. In contrast, 40-45% of Caucasian samples of Western Europe origin carry at least one short allele.

While East Asian cultures have a higher genetic risk, they have a lower **prevalence** of depression.

Gene-culture co-evolution explains that collective cultural values provide buffers from stress in groups with more genetic vulnerabilities to illness. Collectivism fine-tunes the environment so that genetic vulnerabilities are not as damaging to groups.

The authors gathered evidence about the frequency of the short and long alleles of 5-HTT and depression prevalence from 124 studies. Twenty-nine countries representing a mixture of individualism and collectivism values were evaluated.

The authors show a correlation for the first time between the values of individualism-collectivism and expression of the serotonin transporter gene. The field of **cultural neuroscience** is rapidly developing.

Note to the teacher:

> Gene-environment co-evolution is an evolutionary explanation for behavior for Paper 1 and is an example of research about the dimension of culture, individualism-collectivism.

## Cognitive level of analysis: The theory about cognitive style and depressive schemas

Aaron Beck, the founder of cognitive therapy, writes that thoughts are primarily responsible for how we feel and behave (Engler, 2007). Negative cognitive style is a *risk factor* for developing depressive symptoms.

The **cognitive triad**, thoughts about the self, the world, and the future, are the result of cognitive **schemas**. Schemas develop in the context of our experiences and often mirror the schemas of significant others, particularly parents. Schemas are the rules and beliefs that guide behavior.

Schemas of persons with depression are negative and pessimistic. Beck divides thoughts into *automatic* or *controlled*. Automatic beliefs occur just below one's surface awareness and are more difficult to change than conscious controlled thoughts. Destructive self-monologues are examples of automatic thoughts in depressed persons, such as "things are never going to work out because it has always been this way in the past."

The automatic thoughts of people with depression are full of **cognitive distortions**. One kind of distortion magnifies problems, making things worse than they are in reality. An example of magnification is "anything less than an A on a test is a failure; I will never go to college and have a good future." Another cognitive distortion is **dichotomous thinking**, or thinking in extremes. An example of dichotomous thinking is "I am either a total failure or a complete success."

Negative and pessimistic cognitive distortions drive a depressed person's cognitive triad. A person with depression believes he or she is incapable of managing life, sees the world as difficult and harsh, and views the future with pessimism.

Hundreds of studies confirm that cognition is a risk factor correlated with depression. Research clarifies the role of cognition in predicting depression. **Cognitive style**, **brooding**, and **rumination** are the risk cognitions. Rumination means to constantly think about a problem. The pathways are illustrated next.

1. Negative emotions → cognitive style or brooding → depression
2. Life stressors → rumination → depression.

Cognitions are the middle men and are good targets for prevention programs seeking to lower the risk for depression.

## Cognitive Level of Analysis: Two correlation studies showing that cognition is a risk factor for depression

Cognition plays a clear role in how someone's negative emotions, an inborn temperament, turn into depressive symptoms (Arger, Sanchez, Simonson, & Mezulis, 2012).

Young adults filled out self-report questionnaires about negative emotion and three cognitive attributes thought to translate the negative emotions into depressive symptoms, **cognitive style**, **brooding**, and **rumination** after a stressor.

Correlations showed that participants with negative emotions, who also brooded and had a negative cognitive style, were most vulnerable to depression.

Researchers concluded that brooding and negative cognitive style mediated the negative emotion.

A second study clarified the role of **rumination** as a predictor of depressive symptoms (Michl, McLaughlin, Shepherd, & Nolen-Hoeksema, 2013). Rumination was not significant in the Arger, et al. (2012) study and needed investigation.

The authors believed that rumination was important as a specific mediator of stressful events that led to depressive symptoms.

Adolescents and adults filled out self-report questionnaires about social stressors, rumination, and depressive symptoms twice over one year.

Correlations showed that stressful life events were correlated with rumination, and that the greater the rumination, the greater the correlation between rumination and depressive symptoms.

## Sociocultural level of analysis: Techno-brain burnout: Internet use, stress, and depression

Internet use has positive and negative affects on human behavior and is part of a major cultural shift in human interaction. Internet use increases some skills and even improves IQ scores, but it comes with a price— increased stress. Constant stress causes changes in adrenal functioning that affects the brain and increases one's risk for depression.

The solution is not to get rid of the Internet. It is, however, a tool that has become a lifestyle for many, with major consequences. Computers can make life easier, such as shopping on Amazon, buying airline tickets, connecting with out-of-town family members, and finding psychology studies. Students should, however, consider the effects of technology on their lives.

### Theory of Knowledge link

A good TOK discussion might examine the following questions as the class reads the rest of the material in this section.

What is the difference between normal Internet use and excessive use that appears addictive? How has technology affected learning? In what ways does technology contribute to stress and depression? In what ways do people substitute Internet use for real life relationships and what are the consequences?

Thinking about technology is challenging because we are living in the midst of it. Imagine what the human mind was like before the written word. Everything had to be remembered. The first printing press probably had critics claiming the written word would end excellent memories.

The concept **neuroplasticity** reminds us that the brain changes in response to the environment. Young developing brains are the most vulnerable to changes, especially changes affecting the thinking parts of the brain. Each era of information ushered in different underlying brain processing. Information sharing started with storytelling, then changed to the written word, to television, and then to the computer and mobile phones. It is safe to say that brains in the computer era are different from brains of the past. Today's students grew up with computers and cell phones and do not know of a world without them.

An insightful quasi-experiment using **fMRI** to compare the brains of people who had never used a computer with the brains of people using computers regularly provides a frame of reference for considering the effects of technology use on behavior (Small & Vorgan, 2008).

The aim of the study was to examine neuroplastic changes before and after Internet use. Two groups first participated in a control condition that involved reading simulated book text. One group was computer savvy and the other had no previous experience. Brain activity specific to text reading could be subtracted from the scans collected during computer use. The brain activity for both groups was similar when reading text.

Next, both groups started an Internet search task. The scans showed different brain activity. A specific neural network in the dorsolateral prefrontal cortex was recruited in the computer savvy group. This brain area is associated with decision-making, integrating complex information, thoughts, and sensations, as well as working memory. Scans from computer naive participants did not show the same brain activation.

To train the brain, all participants conducted an Internet search each day for five days. After five days, the group without computer experience showed the same brain activity as the computer savvy group.

Modern brains are exposed to technology for long periods of time. Adolescents ages eight to eighteen get an average of 8.5 hours of technology stimulation every day, including television, video and DVD movies, video games, mobile phones, and computers.

What are some potential consequences of so much technology stimulation? Small and Vorgan (2008) write that constant computer exposure has trained the brain to be in a state of **continuous partial attention** where people are always busy, monitoring the Internet and the phone for bits of information but never really focusing on one task. Multitasking is different and its purpose is to improve efficiency. Continuous partial attention keeps people alert for *any* contact, such as news alerts, an email, or a text message. Everything is in one's peripheral attention.

*Stress increases when someone is in a state of continuous partial attention.* People "no longer have time to reflect, contemplate or make thoughtful decisions. Instead they exist in a sense of constant crisis— on alert for a new contact or bit of exciting news or information at any moment" (p. 47).

A person's sense of control is correlated with the size of the hippocampus, and a smaller hippocampus is correlated with emotional instability. Losing a sense of control may be a consequence of long term "continuous partial attention."

Fatigue, irritability, and distractedness are reported from heavy technology users. Small and Vorgan believe that techno-brain burnout is epidemic. The stress of constant alertness signals the fight and flight system and the adrenal glands continually produce the stress hormone **cortisol**.

Unfortunately, cortisol can damage the brain, particularly the developing brain. Teenager's brain are in a phase of tremendous growth in areas related to thinking. High cortisol levels can contribute to **depression** and change the neural circuits in brain areas such as the hippocampus, needed for memory and emotional stability.

## Sociocultural level of analysis: Two studies about Internet use and depression

A growing body of research correlates Internet overuse and **depression**, relationship problems, and poor physical health. Internet addiction is identified as needing further study by the DSM-5 committee for possible later inclusion into the diagnostic manual. Pathological Internet use increases the risk of developing depression (Lam & Peng, 2010). Pathology means "disease causing," and pathological overuse of the Internet means that someone is addicted to its use. Males have the highest rates of Internet addiction, but excessive Internet use by females is increasing. Internet addiction is most studied in East Asian samples, but new research confirms the findings in Western samples.

Lam and Peng ran a correlation study using a random sample of 1618 students from a database of all Chinese high school students in Guangzhou, China aged thirteen to eighteen. Data were gathered with several questionnaires, such as The Internet Addiction Test. One example of a question is "How often do you feel depressed, moody, or nervous when you are off-line, which goes away once you are back online?"

Results included the following.
1. Pathological Internet use negatively affects mental health.
2. Students identified as pathological Internet users have a one and a half times greater risk for developing depression than students with normal use.
3. Students starting out free of mental health problems can develop depression after pathological Internet use begins.

Lam and Peng were the first to gather data over a long time-period, following up with students for nine months. Their study confirmed similar conclusions from cross-sectional studies gathering data at one time-period.

Study results could aid prevention efforts by identifying young people with the greatest risk for developing mental health problems.

A second correlation study confirms the relationship between Internet addiction and depression using adolescents and adults ages sixteen to fifty-one from the United Kingdom as the sample (Morrison & Gore, 2010).

Online questionnaires measured participant Internet use with the Beck Depression Inventory, separating non-addicted users (NA) from Internet addicts (IA).

Results included the following.
1. Internet addiction is real and must be taken seriously. About 2% of the population is addicted to the Internet, or two out of every one hundred people.
2. Participants reporting high levels of depressive symptoms say they are dependent on the Internet.

3. IA participants were more likely to use Internet sites serving as substitutes for face-to-face social relationships, such as online games, chat rooms, or community sites, than NA users.
4. NA users do not score high on depression inventories but for the subgroup of the population identified as Internet addicts, excessive Internet use is a warning sign for depression.

The authors know their study does not predict a specific pathway for the correlation. Does the Internet put people at risk for depression, or are depressed people attracted to online lives? Future research should clarify the pathway, but the relationship is alarming.

# Chapter 8

# Analyze etiologies of two mental disorders: Anorexia Nervosa (AN)

Use the same **risk model** approach to consider etiologies of **anorexia nervosa** (AN) introduced in the last chapter about etiologies of depression. One factor is unlikely to explain AN. The etiologies of AN, bulimia nervosa (BN), and binge-eating disorder (BED), new to DSM-5, are different, so the following list is specific to AN.

## A list of factors that increase the risk of AN
Biological level of analysis:
Genes
Appetite and weight regulation imbalance in the hypothalamus
Neurotransmitters, including serotonin, norepinephrine, and dopamine are examples.
Neuropeptides, which are similar to neurotransmitters and increase (Neuropeptide Y) or decrease (Cholecystokinin and leptin) appetite.
Temperament

Cognitive level of analysis:
Cognitive factors, such as attentional biases toward food

and body related cues, cognitive distortions such as dichotomous thinking

Perfectionism

Reward sensitivity, which means needing a higher reward, meaning they are more sensitive to rewards and praise than people without AN and continue a rewarded behavior even if exhausted.

**Sociocultural level of analysis:**

Media portrayals of cultural attitudes toward thinness

Family interaction

Social learning, including modeling from parents and low self-efficacy

Peer groups, such as sororities

Note to the teacher:

> I start this unit with the NOVA film "Dying to be Thin," available from www.pbs.org. The film is a good summary of anorexia and bulimia. Teachers selecting the sport psychology option can link sport psychology and mental health. The film discusses how ballet dancers have a higher risk of anorexia and highlights exercise addiction.

Examples of etiologies from the three levels of analysis are genes, cognitive style, and media. The levels of analysis interact in complicated ways, so use the bidirectional model outlined in chapter 1 to organize them. The best answers to exam questions asking for one etiology include the interaction with other etiologies, with the focus on one of the student's choice.

## Biological level of analysis: Genetic factors

Genes are important risk factors for AN, but they do not work alone, clearly fitting into a biopsychosocial model (Trace, Baker, Penas-Lledo, & Bulik, 2013). As of 2013, forty-three genes potentially contribute to AN, accounting for approximately 40% to 60% of the risk. *Genetic risk is complicated by the many pathways genes take to affect behavior, so tolerate uncertainty and avoid oversimplification.*

The exact contribution of genes to AN is hard to pinpoint because genes fit into an interactive model with cognitive and sociocultural factors. Family inheritance for AN is well documented, and first-degree relatives are eleven times more likely to have AN. The challenge is to discover which genes stand out as important. Genes related to serotonin, dopamine, opioids, appetite regulation, food intake, and weight regulation are studied, but so far nothing has surfaced as prominent. Studies suffer from inconsistency, lack of replication, and small sample sizes, so conclusions are tentative at best.

*Scientists have at least concluded that genes related to AN do not work alone, so it is best to study them along with cognitive and sociocultural factors related to gene expression.* Genes affect behavior through many pathways that include the following.

1. **Gene by environment interactions** (rGE) are correlations showing how a genetic risk influences a person's environment, meaning "environmental exposure is influenced by genetic factors" (p. 605-6). Three ways for genes to affect a person's environment are active, passive, and evocative interactions. A **passive rGE** occurs when a parent contributes both genes and an environment for a child. The child is a passive recipient

of both, yet their behavior is affected greatly because they inherit the genetic risk and are exposed to parental behavior. An **active rGE** implies that a child's behavior is important to the correlation. For example, girls with a genetic risk for AN might seek out media about cultural values of thinness, thus actively seeking certain kinds of environments (Mazzeo & Bulik, 2009). An **evocative rGE** also implies a child's behavior is important, and occurs when a genetic risk for a behavior, such as a certain temperament, helps create an environment that evokes, or stirs up, behavior from the parent (Trace, et al., 2013).

2. **Gene X environment interactions** (GxE) are correlations showing how genes express differently in different environments. Two ways that GxE affects gene expression are when an environment enhances or buffers gene expression. For example, most girls viewing media idolizing cultural values for slimness do not develop AN, but the risk may be enhanced for those with the risk genes. In addition, stress free environments may buffer, or make someone more resilient, to AN. Recall that Caspi et al. (2003) used gene X environment interactions to study genes and depression.

3. **Gene X gene interactions** (GxG) are correlations showing how a gene interacts with other genes to increase the risk of a behavior (Trace, et al., 2013). For example, people with both one short allele of 5-HT and a long allele of MAOA have eight times the risk for AN. The interaction has a greater effect than it does on its own, called a synergistic effect.

4. **Epigenetics**, meaning that outside factors, such as stress or a poor diet, affect genes and alters their expression. The DNA changes are caused by environmental factors.

Few studies examine epigenetic factors in AN and they focus on abnormal DNA methylation. Normal DNA methylation helps to silence genes and abnormal methylation can result in the inactivation of genes that should be expressed, among other things (Australian Academy of Science, 2006). Many recommendations for future research about epigenetic factors include the effects of maternal diets, stress, and under or over eating (Trace, et al., 2013). Folate, a B vitamin, is one nutrient required for normal DNA methylation. Green vegetables and oranges are two foods containing folate.

Mazzeo and Bulik (2009) give some interesting research examples of rGE.

A **passive rGE correlation** exists between parental models and child disordered eating behavior. For example, studies show that mother's *comments and complaints about their own weight* are correlated with the esteem of their fourth and fifth grade children as well as the concern level that their daughters have about their own weight. It is a passive GXE correlation because these parents pass on genes to their children *and* provide an environment. The children get what Mazzeo and Bulik call a "double dose" of risk factors for eating disorders without doing anything.

An **evocative rGE correlation** also contributes to AN. **Perfectionism** is one example. Although temperament is influenced by genetic factors, a person's temperament also influences how a person interacts with the environment. Research shows that persons with perfectionist temperaments *seek out demanding environments and hold themselves to very high standards*. These persons seek evaluations from others about their performance. Perfectionist persons "evoke" comments from others, and even positive responses from another reinforces a perfectionist personality. In addition, MZ twin research, meaning identical twins research, on AN and BN shows that sometimes one twin receives more critical evaluation from parents. Although both twins may carry a genetic predisposition for eating disorders, only the one twin expresses it, possibly one with a temperament that evokes more criticism from the parent.

Media is one **active GXE correlation** contributing to AN. All girls do not develop eating disorders, although most are exposed to western media idolizing thinness. Girls with a genetic vulnerability for eating disorders might actively seek out media about thinness that reinforces negative views of their own body shape. One study found that girls whose eating disorder symptoms increased over a sixteen-month time-period also reported reading more fashion magazines during that time. In addition, research suggests that girls with genetic vulnerabilities to eating disorders actively select peer groups with the same ideals. European-American girls in sororities have high rates of eating disorders symptoms. Girls in sororities have significantly greater eating disorder symptoms than girls not in sororities after a three-year period.

Research correlating genes with the environments in which they express can help health professionals design prevention programs.

## Cognitive level of analysis: Research about cognitive style

Two types of cognitive factors increase the risk for eating disorders, **attentional biases** toward food and body image, and **cognitive styles** that distort reality (Keel, 2005).

One quasi-experiment compared cognitive styles, specifically information processing biases, of girls with AN and BN with normal controls (Southgate, Tchanturia, & Treasure, 2008).

Cognitive style stems from the temperament that probably interacts with genes.

Cognitive styles predict eating disorder symptoms (Southgate, et al., 2008). Persons diagnosed with AN have obsessive-compulsive personalities, meaning they are perfectionistic, preoccupied with details and order, and have rigid thinking. These personality traits are correlated with inflexibility on cognitive tests. In addition, persons with AN perform better on cognitive tasks requiring local cognitive processing as opposed to global cognitive processing, meaning they pay more attention to detail than to the larger picture. In contrast, persons with BN are impulsive, a trait correlated with binging and purging.

The aim of the study was to examine information processing biases toward *impulsivity* or *efficiency* in persons with an eating disorder as compared to normal controls. Persons with AN were predicted to show the greatest efficiency and persons with BN were predicted to show the greatest impulsivity.

The study is the first to collect data by continuums where *accuracy,* meaning efficiency and perfectionistic processing, at a cognitive task was at one extreme and *speed*, meaning impulsivity, was at the other extreme. Data was gathered through the Matching Familiar Figures Test (MFFT), a demanding task where persons are shown a target picture, a single picture of a familiar object. Then one at a time, eight other similar pictures are shown. Only one is identical to the target picture. Persons must identify the correct match. When the first target picture is correctly matched, the person moves on to the next target picture until all are correctly identified. If an incorrect response is given, the person is asked to try again. Participants in this study were told that both speed and accuracy were measured, but that neither was valued over the other.

The sample included sixty females from the U.K, twenty with AN, fourteen with BN, and twenty-six normal controls, aged sixteen to fifty-seven. All AN and BN participants met the DSM-IV criteria for an eating disorder.

One finding showed that persons with AN were significantly more efficient than controls, supporting the prediction that persons with AN pay more attention to detail. Researchers claim that the findings support knowledge about the clinical symptoms of AN. Self-starvation is correlated with cognitive deficits. Persons with AN suffer from "hyperarousal" where "individuals are often so focused on maintaining their maladaptive behaviors they are unable to see the 'bigger picture' and the severe consequences these behaviors have on their life" (p. 225).

The experiment needs replication, as it is the first study to use a continuum to gather data. In addition, it was impossible to make the researcher administering the MFFT blind to each participant group. It was obvious who made up the AN group. Standardized instructions helped minimize experimenter bias.

## Cognitive level of analysis: A second cognitive style study

A growing body of research confirms cognitive style as a risk factor for AN. One quasi-experiment investigated **cognitive flexibility** as a specific type of cognitive style (Tchanturia et al., 2011).

Cognitive flexibility refers to adapting to changes, and persons with AN have poor flexibility. One study prediction was that persons with AN would perform more poorly on a task measuring the ability to learn new rules as compared to controls without AN. Adapting to change was operationalized in the experiment as the ability to learn new rules.

Participants took the Brixton Spatial Anticipation Test, where the position of a blue colored circle changed for each trial. A rule must be anticipated to figure out the next position of the circle. The ability to anticipate the rule was measured by the number of errors on the test.

Results supported the prediction. Persons with AN had significantly more errors, meaning less flexibility, than controls. The authors think poor cognitive flexibility is an enduring trait of persons with AN, and one factor that maintains the disorder.

*Cognitive inflexibility is now considered a biomarker for eating disorder, meaning that it is a biologically based temperament predisposing some people to a cognitive style that contributes to eating disorder.*

Note to the teacher:

> The National Institute of Health's objections to DSM-5 include the use of self-reported symptoms rather than biomarkers for diagnosis. Cognitive inflexibility is not currently listed as a part of the DSM-5 AN category, but biomarkers might improve the accuracy of future diagnoses.

## Sociocultural level of analysis: Media

Anyone thinking that media is not a risk factor for developing disordered eating should read Anne Becker's research. Higher rates of disordered eating and increased negative body image occurred after the introduction of television to Fiji in the 1990s (Becker, Burwell, Gillian, Herzog, & Hamberg, 2002).

A large body of research shows that the risk of eating disorders increases after exposure to western culture.

Isolating the effects of television on behavior are difficult because control conditions without exposure are rare. Fijian adolescent girls were the perfect solution because television access was limited before 1995. In addition, traditional Fijian culture values hearty eating habits and robust figures.

Was exposure to western television a risk factor for developing disordered eating behavior despite traditional cultural values?

Quantitative data, using a field experiment, and qualitative data, using an interview, were collected.

First, a field experiment tested the incidence of disordered eating in 1995 before exposure to television and again in 1998 after three years of western television. Data for the field experiment were collected through a self-report questionnaire, a modification of the EAT-26, about attitudes toward eating. Most of this data were analyzed with correlations.

Second, semi-structured interviews collected narratives, or important stories, covering a range of eating attitudes from the 1998 sample. The narratives reflected opinions about diet and weight control about traditional Fijian values. Important themes were identified through content analysis.

All ethnic Fijian adolescent girls from two schools in Nadroga, Fiji were in the sample. The 1995 sample included sixty-three girls, with a mean age of 17.3. The 1998 sample included sixty-five girls with a mean age of 16.9.

The results include the following.

1. Field experiments had several important findings. First, a significant difference was found between disordered eating scores on the EAT-26 between the 1995 and 1998 samples. Second, a significant difference was found between the 1995 and 1998 samples about using self-induced vomiting to diet. No one in 1995 sample used self-induced vomiting to diet but by 1998, 11.3% of the girls did. Third, 74% of the 1998 sample said they sometimes felt too fat. There was a significant correlation between feeling too fat and dieting.
2. Interesting themes were identified from the interviews. First, the girls admired the television characters and 83% said that television changed the way they and their friends felt about their body type. Second, 40% felt they had a better chance at career advancement if they were slimmer.

The authors conclude that television plays a significant role in changing values toward body shape and eating behaviors. The following excerpt from the narratives is an example of the changed body image: 'When I look at the characters on TV, the way they act on TV and I just look at the body, the figure of that body, so I say "look at them, they are thin and they all have this figure", so I myself want to become like that, to become thin.' (p. 513).

Limitations of the study include the following.

1. Official diagnoses of eating disorders were not part of the study. Although it is not known if these girls had an official eating disorder, the EAT-26 scores worry the authors.
2. Were the samples comparable? The same girls were not in both samples so it is unknown if the 1998 sample had disordered eating before the arrival of television. The authors feel it was unlikely that these girls had disordered eating before 1995 because there was only one report of AN in Fiji before that time.

## Sociocultural level of analysis: A second media study

Research continues to show that media is an important etiology for disordered eating. Even indirect exposure to media through parental and friend use is a risk (Becker, et al., 2011).

Is both direct contact with media, meaning individual, and indirect contact with media, meaning its use by important social networks, related to disordered eating?

Fiji was a good place to continue research about media and disordered eating. Many Fijians kept traditional cultural beliefs, including valuing larger body sizes. At the same time, disordered eating increased in younger generations after access to western media.

All girls ages fifteen to twenty attending school were in the sample. Self-report questionnaires gathered data about media use. Individual direct use was measured by personal and household access to television and video viewing and electronic media use. Indirect social network use was measured by parental and friend use of television and video viewing, the use of DVD players, Internet access, CD or MP3 player, and mobile phones.

Correlations showed significant relationships between disordered eating and media use by social networks, and the conclusion was independent of the effects of direct use. *Indirect exposure may be even more important than individual use.*

Correlations do not identify causal pathways, so media could affect behavior, behavior could affect media viewing, and heavy viewing girls could be attracted to heavy viewing peers. The argument that media does not affect behavior applied only to previous studies about direct exposure where people had control over choices. The girls in this study did not choose their indirect exposure, so personal characteristics were not a relevant pathway. The study is intriguing and raises serious questions about health in a global society ever more dependent on visual media.

# Chapter 9

## Discuss cultural and gender variations in prevalence of disorders

Be careful with the term "variation." "Variation" is fine as long as it is not interpreted as a contrast to a "real" western disorder or a disorder studied with just males or females. Prevalence rates failing to take culture and gender into account run the risk of *over or under-representing* the actual occurrence. For example, **stereotypes** about female gender roles may cause overrepresentation of females in depression prevalence rates. In addition, males may be underrepresented in eating disorder prevalence rates because they are rarely included in research samples.

### Why is it hard to know about culture and prevalence?

Cultural variations in the prevalence of mental illness are hard to know.

*Data must be comparable for accuracy.* Gathering credible data is difficult, so all current estimates are tentative and possibly inaccurate (Marsella & Yamada, 2007). Survey is the primary research method for gathering prevalence data and its interpretation is affected by the biases of those collecting the data, the source of the data, and the reliability and validity of the survey questions. Given differences in the expression and course of mental illnesses across cultures, to what extent is any comparison possible?

Studying prevalence within an individual country is challenging enough with the different regions and types of people involved. Comparing countries is even more demanding. *Researchers cannot study variations or say that one group has more mental illness than another without running a cross-cultural study where numerous cultures are surveyed and compared in a meaningful way.*

Marsella and Yamada recommend five strategies for planning and running a comparable survey.

1. Categories for the comparison study should come from the results of ethnographies, meaning observation studies of cultural practices. DSM categories do not automatically apply to others.
2. All words and concepts for the comparisons must be clearly defined.
3. All assessments must measure symptoms that are meaningful for each culture.
4. Case examples must be equivalent across cultures. For example, if people from different cultures report sleep difficulties, low energy, and sadness, do they all have depression?
5. A clearly defined baseline must be established for **normality** and **abnormality**.

## A World Health Organization (WHO) survey about culture and prevalence

One survey study about cross-cultural prevalence rates for mental illness is the WHO (2004) survey of the prevalence, severity, and unmet needs of people with mental disorders across fourteen countries. Marsella and Yamada's (2007) recommendations were challenges for all aspects of designing the study, collecting data, and analysis.

Surveys were collected from 60,463 participants in fourteen countries (WHO, 2004). The countries were Belgium, Colombia, France, Germany, Italy, Japan, Lebanon, Mexico, Netherlands, Nigeria, People's Republic of China (in Beijing and Shanghai), Spain, Ukraine, and the U.S. Efforts were made to recruit other samples, but only countries with money to fund the study could participate.

Data were gathered through a face-to-face household survey. The survey was a structured interview using the WHO Composite International Diagnostic Interview (CIDI). It was administered by trained lay persons. The sample came from a variety of databases within each country, such as national registers and telephone directories. The CIDI gathered the prevalence of many disorders, including depression, phobias, PTSD, and eating disorders. The survey excluded severe disorders such as schizophrenia.

Categories of mental illnesses were formed from the DSM-IV. The definitions were declared reliable and valid, though the article does not say how reliability and validity were established.

Results showed that prevalence over a twelve-month period varied a great deal, from 4.3% in Shanghai to 26.4% in the U.S. The incidence for having all disorders was:

Belgium-12%
Colombia-17.8%
France-18.4%
Germany- 9.1%
Italy- 8.2%
Japan-8.8%

Lebanon-16.9%
Mexico-12.2%
Netherlands-14.8%
Nigeria- 4.7%
People's Republic of China, Shanghai-4.3% and Beijing-
 9.1%
Spain-9.2%
Ukraine-20.4%
United States-16.3%

The prevalence of mild disorders varied from 1.8% in Shanghai to 9.2% in the U.S. The prevalence of moderate disorders ranged from a low of 1.4% in Shanghai to 9.4% in the U.S. The prevalence of severe disorders ranged from 0.4% in Nigeria to 7.7% in the U.S.

Anxiety disorders were the most prevalent of the disorders in all but the Ukraine, where mood disorders were most prevalent. Mood disorders were the second most prevalent disorder except in Nigeria and Beijing, where substance abuse disorders ranked second.

The amount of persons with disorders receiving treatment in the twelve months before the interview varied a great deal. Nigeria reported the lowest amount of treatment, 0.8% and the U.S. reported the highest level, 15.3%. Many people do not receive any treatment. Up to 50.3% of the severe cases in less developed countries and up to 85.4% of severe cases in developed countries received no treatment. Some of the treatment resources are going to less severe cases. The WHO recommends that treatment resources be allocated so that more serious mental health cases get treatment. The WHO realizes that it is easy to suggest reallocation and hard to do so effectively.

For example, it does it make sense to leave mild cases untreated, as many with mild cases become serious if left untreated?

Survey limitations include the following.

1. Survey response was widely varied, with some of the response rates too low for an accepted standard. Cross-national comparisons may be distorted.
2. Some surveys did not include certain disorders considered irrelevant for particular countries, making comparisons difficult. The CIDI was standardized in the West, so "performance ... could be worse in other parts of the world either because the concepts or phrases used to describe mental syndromes are less consonant (in agreement) with cultural concepts than in developed Western countries or because absence of a tradition of free speech and anonymous public opinion surveying causes greater reluctance to admit emotional or substance-abuse problems than in developed West countries" (p. 2587).
3. Schizophrenia and other severe disorders were not included in the survey. The WHO decided that persons with schizophrenia typically met the criteria for other disorders on the survey, such as mood or anxiety disorders, and were captured in these statistics.

A strength of the WHO survey is consistency with other surveys showing that mental disorders are prevalent around the world and frequently not treated.

Marsella and Yamada (2007) criticize the WHO survey. Reported variations may reflect real rates but the validity of the interviews cannot go unchallenged. DSM-IV categories do not include culture-bound disorders relevant to each individual culture. *Prevalence rates are distorted if interview respondents are not talking about the same thing.* Should we conclude that Chinese persons experience little stress? In addition, any study is designed in line with a researcher's *values*. Never assume that a researcher's values represent an "authority."

What conclusions can we draw about prevalence of mental illness across culture?
1. Designing a credible survey with relevance for all cultures is almost impossible and the reported results are tentative.
2. Cultures experience mental illness in unique ways.
3. Mental health services are not reaching everyone needing help.

The next section about gender and eating disorder prevalence contains two survey studies (Marques, et al., 2011; Alegria, et al. 2007) investigating both gender and culture variations to use for additional research in an essay or questions asking for cultural difference in prevalence for one disorder.

## Background ideas for considering gender variations in prevalence of mental disorders

Important points for considering gender variations in prevalence of mental illness show the scope of the issues.

1. Males and females have similar overall rates of mental illness but vary according to specific disorders (Lips, 2005). Women have higher prevalence rates of depression, eating disorders, and specific phobias such as agoraphobia. Males have higher rates of antisocial behavior, substance abuse,

and childhood disorders, such as autism. Avoid thinking that females are not substance abusers or that males do not have eating disorders or depression. Perhaps male and female expressions of the disorders are different and classification systems inadequate to show the reality of male depression and female alcoholism. For example, men are typically excluded from samples in eating disorders studies, even though they make up about 40% of people with binge eating disorders (Keel, 2005).

2. Gender **stereotypes** may affect expectations of how someone should cope with distress (Lips, 2005).
3. A "politics of diagnosis" reflects gender stereotypes and role expectations, and "sex-biases built into diagnostic categories may well influence perceptions of whether women and men are psychologically healthy" (Lips, 2005, p. 373). Psychiatry is dominated by males, and biases may surround diagnostic categories using male behavior as the "norm." Females behaving in line with their socialization may be diagnosed as abnormal. Do males and females reporting similar symptoms to a doctor get the same diagnosis and treatment?
4. **Stress** is a factor (Lips, 2005). Both males and females experience stressful events, such as accidents or divorce, but *women experience stress differently than men and have more lifelong stressors*, such as poverty and the responsibility for children.
5. Questionnaires are popular research tools where participants select all stressful events that apply, but some may not accurately estimate male and female experiences (Lips, 2005). Are lists of stressful

events biased toward male experiences? Do men have more positive life changing experiences than women? Could women respond more strongly to stressful events? Sometimes lists of stressful life events fail to include circumstances important to women, such as rape and difficulties managing child care. In addition, women tend to rate experiencing stressors at greater intensities than men. One questionnaire was developed to study sexist behavior, a stressor females endure more frequently than males. The Schedule of Sexist Events included situations such as degrading jokes and sexual harassment at work. Half of the participants reported being picked on, threatened, and even hit because they were female. Forty percent said they were denied a raise or promotion because they were a woman.

## Gender variations in prevalence of depression

Females have three times more depression than males.

What explains the large difference? Women experience more stressors and experience stress differently than men (Nolan-Hoeksema, 2004).

Females are more vulnerable to depression because they have more social stressors than males. Two particular life events are correlated with higher rates of depression. First, women experience greater amounts of childhood sexual assault, which is related to developing depression in adulthood. Second, women tend to have lower social status than men and often do not have a voice in decision-making.

Interpersonal orientation is the only aspect of self-concept relevant to depression rates. Females are more concerned with relationships than males. Females place less emphasis on their own needs and are more vulnerable to depression when relationships are troubled or end.

To complicate matters, females ruminate, meaning to think over problems, more than males. Rumination increases the risk for depression.

Last, females may be more biologically reactive to stress. One interesting theory that needs more research is that sex hormones affect the stress system. Sex hormones have not been shown to directly affect mood. Females experience more social stressors and are more prone to disturbances in the HPA axis, referring to the cascade of events that occur in the hypothalamus, pituitary gland, and adrenal cortex after someone experiences a stressor. Are sex hormones part of the puzzle?

Males may be underrepresented in depression statistics, possibly experiencing depression differently. Six million men in the U.S. experience depression each year (NIMH, 2008). Men and women show standard symptoms, but research suggests that they experience and cope with depression differently. Females talk more openly about emotions than men and seek health care more frequently. Men report more physical symptoms, such as sleep difficulties and irritability. Some researchers believe the DSM category is inadequate to describe male depression. For example, men are more likely to be diagnosed with substance use disorder. Is substance use really a symptom of depression? In addition, men are more likely to throw themselves into their jobs or engage in reckless behavior than females, perhaps other signs of male depression.

## Gender variations in prevalence of eating disorders

Statistics show that females have most of the eating disorders, but a discussion about male disordered eating raises concerns about diagnosis. The DSM-5 categories do not offer insight about gender issues.

Females have anorexia at rates three times greater than males. Males account for 10% of eating disorders, though they are most likely to have binge-eating disorder (BED) when they have one (Keel, 2005). Most of the research on eating disorders uses female samples, so psychologists do not know as much about the male experience. For example, males account for 40% of BED but are generally excluded from samples studying it.

Keel raises some good questions about males and eating disorders. Do the findings from studies using females participants apply to males? Are some risk factors for eating disorders specific to males that are unknown from studying females? Do males show symptoms of eating disorders that differ from those women display? If so, then perhaps males are underrepresented in eating disorder statistics.

Keel thinks that there are some risk factors specific to men needing more research.
1. Males are more likely to be overweight or obese before the beginning of their eating disorder.
2. Participating in **sports** that require low body weight, such as wrestling, or a low percentage of body fat, such as body building, are factors.
3. Homosexuality is a risk factor.
4. Pursuing an extreme masculine role may be a risk factor, called **reverse anorexia**. Reverse anorexia is when

males perceive their bodies as too small, even when body building has greatly increased overall body mass.

## Two survey studies about gender and culture differences in the prevalence of eating disorders in the U.S.

The following study examines *both gender and cultural variations* in the prevalence of eating disorders.

Recent research challenges the widely held notion that only white western women suffer from eating disorders.

Alegria, et al. (2007) conducted *the first study about prevalence rates of eating disorders in Latino ethnic groups living in the U.S.* Some studies suggested Latino females had higher rates of eating disorder than other ethnic minorities, including Asian-Americans and African-Americans. In addition, clarification was needed about the extent to which **acculturation**, meaning to adopt behaviors that represent the norms and values of the dominant culture, accounted for the eating disorders.

Surveys were collected from a sample of 2554 English and Spanish-speaking Latinos living in the U.S. Four Latino subgroups were identified; 868 Mexicans, 495 Puerto Ricans, 577 Cubans, and 614 other Latinos.

Researchers gathered three categories of data for the survey, prevalence rate of eating disorder, acculturation, and Body Mass Index.

Lay persons collected the survey data through structured interviews.

Presence of an eating disorder was determined by DSM-IV criteria. Four eating disorder categories were created; AN, bulimia nervosa (BN), binge-eating disorder (BED), and any binge eating.

Acculturation was measured as being native or foreign born, if one or both parents were born in the U.S., and percentage of one's life spent in the U.S (Alegria, et al., 2007).

Participants were organized into four weight categories based on BMI; underweight, normal weight, overweight, and severely obese.

The results included the following.

1. No one, male or female, met the criteria for AN.
2. Females had higher rates for BN and BED than males, but the differences were insignificant.
3. There was no significant difference in prevalence for BN or BED across ethnic subgroup.
4. Participants under thirty years of age had a significantly higher rate of BN than those over thirty. The prevalence of BED did not vary by age.
5. Acculturation contributes to eating disorder prevalence. Participants living in the U.S. the longest had significantly higher prevalence rates for eating disorders than participants new to the U.S.

Conclusions include the following.

1. Binge eating disorders are a serious health problem for ethnic Latinos living in the U.S.
2. AN is not common in ethnic Latinos living in the U.S. The authors note that results may not be accurate because ethnic Latinos may express AN differently. Future research should include culturally relevant assessments for ethnic groups living in the U.S.

3. The gender differences found in the Latino sample greatly contrasts with gender differences found in white U.S. samples. The lack of a significant difference in male and female ethnic Latinos may be real or the result of a fairly small sample.
4. Rates of eating disorders is increasing in ethnic Latinos. Persons living in the U.S. for more than 70% of their lifetime had the highest lifetime prevalence rates of BN.
5. Highly educated people had the highest rates of BED.

Several weaknesses limit data interpretation. First, the survey was conducted on a small sample, Second, self-reports could have been distorted by recall biases. Third, lay persons conducted the interviews. The authors suggest that longitudinal studies follow up on the results.

A second survey compared gender and culture prevalence of eating disorders across all major ethnic groups in the U.S., including Latinos, Asians, African-Americans, and non-Latino whites (Marques, et al., 2011).

Results were similar to the 2007 study and include the following.
1. AN is uncommon in Latinos and African-Americans.
2. Rates of AN, BN, and binge eating disorder (BED) are similar across all groups for both males and females, Latinos, Asians, African-Americans, and non-Latino whites, contrary to public perceptions that white women have the most cases of AN.
3. BN rates are significantly higher for Latinos, both males and females, and African-Americans females.

4. Even with similar or higher instances of disordered eating, Latinos, African-Americans, and Asians underutilize mental health care services.

Self-reports and recall bias could limit study interpretations. One lesson is that some ethnic groups, for many reasons that need exploration, are not using medical services for eating disorders.

# Chapter 10

## Examine biomedical, individual, and group approaches to treatment

This learning outcome is similar to the next. Assumptions for the different approaches to treatment are provided in this chapter and research on treatments is provided in the next chapter. Just remember, *all treatments affect neurotransmission and neural circuitry, and many treatments end up with the same effects, even if treatment assumptions differ and the pathways to change vary*. Health care providers and patients must decide which approach is the "best fit" or if an **eclectic** approach, meaning a combination of treatments, is needed. Decisions about treatment depend on the situation of the patient as well as the preference of practitioners, which tends to relate to their training.

### Assumptions of a biomedical approach to treatment

Biomedical treatments include drugs, acupuncture, and exercise.

The **Western psychiatric approach** views mental illnesses as diseases that are treated with **drugs**. Treatments "work" if symptoms are reduced. Errors in thinking about western psychiatric treatments lie in several areas (Hecker & Thorpe, 2005). First, it is wrong to assume that biomedical treatments are the only logical treatments for disorders with strong biological abnormalities. Second, it is wrong to assume that if a biomedical treatment reduces symptoms, then psychological factors are not important. The opposite claim is also problematic, that psychological treatments reducing symptoms rule out the importance of biological factors.

The **Traditional Chinese Medicine (TCM) approach** is different, and includes **acupuncture**. Chinese doctors consider the entire person, both physically and psychologically. Chinese doctors ask questions about things that seem unrelated to a person's complaint, such as diet and exercise. Chinese doctors look for patterns of disharmony in the entire system of a person that show general imbalances (Kaptchuk, 1983). *Finding relationships is far more important than determining cause and effect in TCM.* The pattern of disharmony might be maintained by one fundamental problem that seems unrelated to the symptom. For example, food allergies might play a fundamental role in maintaining a number of interrelated symptoms, including depressed mood.

Chinese medicine views a person's physiology as a series of **meridians**. Meridians are bioelectrical impulses, similar to an electrical system, to put it in western terms. "Meridians are the channels or pathways that carry Qi and Blood through the body" (Kaptchuk, 1983, p. 77). **Qi** (Chi) means "energy," the life force (Hammer, 2005). Energy passes through twelve meridians that keep one's physical system in balance (Kaptchuk, 1983). Blood that flows through the meridians is not real blood but "an invisible network that links together all of the fundamental substances and organs" (p. 77). *Meridians connect this interior flow of Qi and Blood with the outer body. This is why acupuncture works.* **Acupuncture**, **Tai Chi**, and **herbal medicines** unblock stagnated Qi and blood flow and restore balance. Acupuncture points on the exterior body are places along meridians where needles are inserted to stimulate Qi and Blood flow within the interior system and unblock stagnations. Tai Chi practice cultivates Qi within the body. Tai Chi practice does this by facilitating a calm strength in the body through the coordination of hands, feet, head, and breathing. Tai Chi improves circulation, balance, and flexibility. It relaxes and strengthens the nervous system and relieves many medical problems such as hypertension, allergies, arthritis, diabetes, **depression**, aggressive feelings, and anxiety.

The goal of Chinese medicine is to create harmony and reestablish balance within the meridians. *Western medicine has no concept similar to Qi* (Hammer, 2005).

TCM "works" when harmony is reestablished. Experiments testing the effectiveness of acupuncture, herbs, and Tai Chi to treat mental disorder use symptom reduction to define "working" because it is expected that experiments track diagnostic symptoms.

The **exercise approach** is beneficial because it makes people feel good for many reasons (Nahas & Sheikh, 2011). Exercise alters the brain and many of the changes are similar to the effects of taking drugs. Changes include altering neurotransmitters, promoting growth in the hippocampus, and lowering cortisol, an important human stress hormone. In addition, exercise promotes social connections and helps people feel in control of their health. Some doctors may not want to prescribe exercise because of low patient motivation—it is recommended as a first line of defense for all patients if doctors provide a structured exercise routine and follow up on progress with counseling. Exercise is defined as "working" if symptoms are reduced in experiments.

## Assumptions of an individual approach to treatment

An **individual approach** refers to one-on-one talking therapy, such as **cognitive therapy**, explained in chapter 7. The long-term goal of cognitive therapy is to restructure thinking styles, which can be altered to some extent in a short period. So, "working" in the short-run is defined as symptom reduction in experiments. Long-term internalization of new behaviors may take longer, so fully achieving the long-term goal may take a longer period of therapy.

## Assumptions of a group approach to treatment

A **group approach** is therapy delivered to more than one person at a time. Many therapies are provided in groups. **Mindfulness-based cognitive therapy** (MBCT) and **group interpersonal therapy** (IPT) are examples of group depression treatments. Again, "working" is usually defined as symptom reduction in experiments, though long-term goals are to learn mindfulness, restructure cognitions, and come to terms with past and present social roles.

A group approach is effective, *as long as the client is enthusiastic about getting therapy in a group setting and has mild to moderate symptoms* (Truax, 2001).

Truax reviewed a meta-analysis on group depression treatment. Forty-eight studies conducted between 1970 and

1998 were reviewed. Cognitive therapy (CT) was preferred for groups in studies. Several findings are important. First, people with depression receiving group psychotherapy improve significantly more than those getting no treatment. Second, there was no significant difference between the progress of depressed persons getting group psychotherapy and those getting individual treatment.

It is no surprise that successful individual approaches also have success in groups. The *client's preference is probably the key* to selecting the right treatment setting. Is the person enthusiastic about group therapy? If not, individual therapy is just as effective.

Why not have others present during therapy (Hecker & Thorpe, 2005)? How can hardworking therapists deliver counseling to everyone needing it? At best, it is only possible to deliver individual therapy to a small number of persons at a time.

Group approaches are beneficial for many reasons. Acceptance by peers and belonging to a group is important, particularly for lonely people. Many therapeutic factors are common to all therapies offered in a group setting. These include creating hope and group closeness, reframing so that people see they are not the only ones with problems, giving information, healing old family issues, developing social skills, modeling another's success, and processing emotions.

Group therapies may become more popular in the future as health care dollars become more limited.

# Chapter 11

# Examine the use of biomedical, individual, and group approaches to the treatment of one disorder: Major depression

## Background for understanding depression treatments

The prevalence of depression is increasing and everyone wants to find the best treatments. The most effective treatment is **prevention**, but depression will continue until global sources of stress are identified and eliminated.

Note to the teacher:

> I call this learning outcome "loaded" because it requires more than the others. Students must prepare for questions about one or a combination of treatment approaches. Many are reviewed so students study a range of available treatments and get a balanced, cross-cultural view.

**Drugs**, including combinations with cognitive therapy or acupuncture, **exercise**, **acupuncture**, individual

**cognitive therapy**, and group **mindfulness-based cognitive therapy** and **interpersonal therapy** are examined.

All the reviewed treatments are effective, so selecting the best one depends on many factors that vary by person. Ensuring that everyone has access to treatment is necessary because untreated mental health problems affect all aspects of a person's life, including the ability to work and maintain stable family relationships.

Any source claiming that a particular treatment is best for everyone with a set of symptoms is guilty of *oversimplification*. Treatment choice depends on many factors, such as the severity of the symptoms, a person's culture, the cause of the problem if one can be identified, and the presence of other mental and/or physical health problems.

## A cross-cultural list of depression treatments

Depression treatments include, but are not limited to the following:

### Biomedical treatments
Drug therapy, such as Prozac
Electroconvulsive therapy
Acupuncture
Herbal medicine, such as St. John's Wort
Diet change
Exercise
Vagus Nerve Stimulation
Transcranial Magnetic Stimulation

Individual treatments
Cognitive therapy (CT)
Mindfulness-based cognitive therapy (MBCT) - A combination of meditation and CT
Interpersonal therapy (IPT)
Guided mastery therapy to raise self-efficacy
Faith healers, shaman, or other culture based community treatments

Group treatments
Family therapy
Marital therapy
Group Psychotherapy

Treatments should have a high degree of **efficacy**, meaning that randomized experiments support a treatment's use. All the studies reviewed in this chapter are part of a body of evidence with high efficacy.

## Some things to consider when evaluating treatments

Researchers are past the point of asking if available treatments are effective, and now study *when* to use treatments and *in what combination*. The following seven points help with evaluating treatment research.

1. Treatment selection should take into account potential benefits versus potential risks.
2. Modern health providers require evidence from randomized experiments, referred to as RCTs, or randomized controlled experiments. "Randomized" means that participants are randomly assigned to

groups. Randomized experiments show that a treatment caused a change to occur. RCTs are studied over limited time frames, typically twelve to sixteen weeks, and symptom reduction is how "working" is defined, even if the theory suggests something else for long-term effectiveness. RCTs have advantages, such as showing cause and effect and using clearly defined samples to control participant variables. Although the clearly defined sample may appear a disadvantage, everyone knows that the point of the studies is to test the treatments and that real life clients are more complicated.
3. Culture affects the perception and acceptance of treatments, even affecting how drugs alter the brain, so cultural relevance is importance for delivering all treatments (Kleinman, 2004).
4. Placebos complicate studying treatments, particularly depression. Whether placebos are ethical is debated, but they serve a purpose and new study designs are better at keeping placebos from interfering with real treatments benefits.
5. It is hard to know if any treatment works in the long run.
6. No one treatment works for everyone. Some people do not respond to any treatment. Some people get better without any formal treatment.
7. To complicate matters, *no studies compare all available treatments, making comparisons difficult.* A study comparing all available treatments is not practical.

## Biomedical Treatment # 1: The antidepressant Prozac

Western psychiatrists often prescribe **antidepressants** as the "first line of defense" against depression, though drugs are sometimes combined with other treatments. Many antidepressants are available and they all affect **neurotransmission** in some way. One type is the SSRIs, the selective serotonin reuptake inhibitors, such as **Prozac**.

Note to the teacher:

> Students sometimes have trouble understanding *risk versus benefit*, an important **ethical consideration**. Avoid extremist views. One place to start is with the film segment about depression from the PBS series "The Secret Life of the Brain". Lauren Slater shares the first ten years of her Prozac use. Lauren's symptoms were severe; So, did the benefits of taking the drug outweigh the risks? The film sparks good discussion.

## The case of Lauren Slater

*Clearly there are people who need drug therapy and benefit from it.*

Consider Lauren Slater's case from the impressive PBS series called "The Secret Life of the Brain". Although the show is older, it is still relevant for introducing students to Prozac's effects on the brain and someone's experiences with the drug. Lauren Slater is featured in the depression segment. Lauren, author of the book "The Prozac Diary," talks candidly about managing severe depression and taking Prozac over the twelve-year period the film covers.

Her experiences might surprise you and elicit your empathy. Those students who believed that drugs are a simple solution now understand differently and those who spoke out against prescription drugs see that drugs can be helpful. Prozac helped Lauren, but as the drugs reduced one set of problems, another set emerged.

After five hospitalizations, Lauren started taking Prozac in 1988, the year Eli Lilly released it (Book Clubs/Reading Guides, 2008). Lauren had an immediate positive benefit. Her symptoms melted away after just five days on the drug and the world was a new and wonderful place. Within a year Lauren was accepted into Harvard and she earned a doctorate in psychology. Lauren married, had a child, and became a therapist. Lauren was one of the first people to take Prozac for over a decade.

Life is never simple. Lauren experienced what patients call **Prozac Poop-Out**, even though "poop outs" can happen with many drugs. Poop-Outs mean that the brain develops a *tolerance* to the drug and its effectiveness diminishes. Here is one limitation of antidepressant drugs, as about one-third of people taking Prozac experience tolerance problems after one year of taking the drug (Harvard Magazine, 2000).

Along with tolerance, Lauren experienced other side effects of taking Prozac, such as a loss of creativity (Book Club/Reading Guides, 2008). Over the first twelve years of taking Prozac, Lauren's doctor raised her dosage from 10 milligrams each day to 80 milligrams, the top limit approved by the U.S. Food and Drug Administration (FDA). Sometimes Lauren's doctor switched her to other types of antidepressant drugs when Prozac was not working at all and her symptoms returned.

The Prozac Diary describes the benefits and the risks of taking an antidepressant. Lauren raises ethical questions about her use of Prozac, such as, "Am I really myself on the drug?" and "Is taking the drug robbing me of important experiences?"

Lauren continued to take the drug because her symptoms were so bad. Lauren's doctor continued to increase her dosage after the film to levels higher than recommended by the FDA. Lauren says she will wait and see what happens. She embraces the reduction of depressive symptoms yet fears the potential increases in side effects, cognitive damage, toxicity, or a time when Prozac does not work at all. Why did Lauren continue to take Prozac? *Because the benefits outweighed the risks.*

When faced with long-term severe depressive symptoms, might the benefits of taking the drugs outweigh its risks? There is much to consider before someone takes an antidepressant. Some people respond to one antidepressant and not another. Some people experience side effects, though SSRIs are generally well tolerated. Some people cannot take drugs at all. Anyone taking a drug must have their symptoms regularly monitored.

Next, let's evaluate Prozac.

## Thinking about Prozac

Antidepressants have been around for a long time and decisions about taking them are complicated. Benefits must outweigh risks.

Risks include the following.
1. One risk is side effects. Check the side effects of any drug at PubMedHealth.
2. A second risk is tolerance to the drug, called Prozac poop-out. Tolerance means that the brain

compensates for the drug's effect. Prozac prevents the reuptake of **serotonin**, making more available at synapses. The brain responds by creating more receptors.
3. Drugs reduce symptoms, which is beneficial, but there is a risk that people do not learn new behaviors without taking action to learn new ways of managing stress.

The primary benefit of taking Prozac is symptom reduction, which makes it possible for people to live more normal day-to-day lives, including working, caring for children, and lessening the risk of suicide.

Antidepressants are most useful for people with moderate to severe depression rather than mild depression (The Royal College of Psychiatrists, n.d.).

Many antidepressants are available, grouped according to how they affect **neurotransmission**. Newer antidepressants are not necessarily more effective than older drugs.
1. Tricyclics, such as Elavil, that prevent serotonin and norepinephrine reuptake
2. MAIOs, such as Nardil, that are monoamine oxidase inhibitors
3. SSRIs, such as **Prozac** and Lexapro, that prevent serotonin reuptake
4. SNRIs, such as Cymbalta, that prevent serotonin and norepinephrine reuptake
5. NASSAs, such as Mirtazapine, that block serotonin and adrenaline receptors, making the substances available at synapses

All available antidepressants lessen depression to some extent. Drugs cannot get approval from the Food and Drug Administration (FDA) unless they perform better than **placebos** in randomized placebo-controlled experiments. Some reports suggest that antidepressants lessen depressive symptoms by 65% compared with a 30% reduction with placebos (The Royal College of Psychiatrists, n.d,). Other researchers report that placebos work as well as antidepressants and are effective up to 47% of the time (Lambert, 2008).

**Prozac** is widely used and the example antidepressant. Many SSRI drugs are on the market and you might recognize some of the others, such as Paxil and Zoloft.

The different SSRI drugs are used in particular circumstances, even though they all fit under the general category of SSRIs.

## Prozac treatment for adolescents

The FDA approved Prozac in 1987. Prozac is still popular even though newer drugs are available. Prozac was a breakthrough because so many patients had trouble tolerating some of the older antidepressants. It was clear by the 1970s that enhancing serotonin (5-HTT) in the brain lessened depression symptoms and a new class of antidepressants was born (eMedExpert, 2012).

*Prozac is the only SSRI approved by the FDA for use in children 8 and older.*

Prozac is a good choice for many reasons, including a low risk for weight gain, mild withdrawal symptoms when someone decides to stop taking the drug, and a lower risk of suicide. The FDA includes warnings about suicide risks for each antidepressant and one place to check these warnings and other important information, including side effects, is PubMedHealth.

The FDA (2012) reports that Prozac performs significantly better than a placebo in numerous randomized placebo-controlled experiments with adults.

What about Prozac's effectiveness with children? The FDA reported that two separate randomized, placebo-controlled experiments testing Prozac on children, one ages eight to thirteen and the other ages thirteen to eighteen, showed that children over eight taking Prozac had fewer depressive symptoms.

Using antidepressants with children is controversial so let's explore research from 2004 to 2009 investigating the effectiveness of Prozac, including comparisons with cognitive therapy. In addition, research shows that Prozac makes important neuroplastic brain changes in adolescents that account for its effectiveness.

*Do not underestimate the risk of suicide in depressed persons.* If suicide risk is high, then the fastest treatment is the best.

## Research examples: The 3 TADS studies: Prozac and its combination with Cognitive Therapy for adolescents

The Treatment for Adolescents with Depression Studies (**TADS**) shows how antidepressant research progresses over time. Each study builds on previous findings. The U.S. National Institute of Health (NIH) funds TADS and aims to study short- and long-term effects of antidepressants and cognitive therapy alone and in combination for depressed teenagers (NIH, 2012). The studies took place between 2004 and 2009.

**TADS I** was conducted at thirteen sites using 439 adolescents between twelve and seventeen years old diagnosed with major depression using the DSM-IV category (TADS Team, 2004).

Participants were randomly assigned in an experiment to get Prozac alone, cognitive therapy alone, combined cognitive therapy and Prozac, or a placebo. The Prozac alone and placebo conditions were double-blind and the other two conditions were not blinded.

Depressive symptoms were rated using the Children's Depression Rating Scale.

The experiment lasted twelve weeks, so TADS I measured *short-term effects*.

Results included the following.
1. The combination Prozac and cognitive therapy groups improved more than the placebo group.
2. Combined Prozac and cognitive therapy was better than either treatment alone.
3. Prozac alone was better than cognitive therapy alone.

The team concluded that combined Prozac and cognitive therapy was the best short-term treatment for adolescent depression. One reason to favor combination treatments is that cognitive therapy helps teenagers learn new ways to manage stress.

**TADS II** examined longer-term treatment effectiveness and safety over thirty-six weeks at thirteen sites in a randomized experiment (TADS Team, 2007).

TADS II used 327 adolescents between the ages of twelve and seventeen with moderate to severe depression. TADS II used the same conditions as the 2004 research.

The placebo group was ended at twelve weeks because researchers could already see its effects.
Results included the following.
1. After twelve weeks, 73% responded positively to combination therapy, 62% to Prozac, and 48% to cognitive therapy.
2. After eighteen weeks, 85% responded positively to combination therapy, 69% to Prozac, and 65% to cognitive therapy.
3. After thirty-six weeks, 86% responded positively to combination therapy, 81% to Prozac, and 81% to cognitive therapy.

The fastest response was the combination treatment. The groups responded about the same at the end of thirty-six weeks. The authors concluded that taking Prozac or combining it with cognitive therapy gave the fastest response. It took longer for cognitive therapy to work and the authors were concerned that *the risks associated with depression, such as suicide, must be treated quickly.* This is a genuine concern and is one benefit that might outweigh the risks associated with taking the drug.

Do the effects of Prozac, cognitive therapy, and their combination last over the long-term? The aim of **TADS III** was to examine effectiveness over a one-year naturalistic follow-up (TADS Team, 2009). TADS III is not an experiment. Experiments testing treatments are difficult to control over long periods of time because confounding variables, such as getting a new job, interfere with the study conditions.

The follow-up study used the Children's Depression Rating Scale to see how the 327 participants in the 2007 TADS II study were doing after one year.

Results included the following.
1. Participants receiving combined Prozac and cognitive therapy had the fastest recovery and the recovery continued over the one-year follow-up.
2. Long-term treatment is better than short-term treatment. Long-term treatment lessens relapse.
3. Adolescents receiving cognitive therapy along with Prozac reported fewer suicide thoughts.

In conclusion, Prozac can be an effective treatment for depression. In addition, it is the only drug with FDA approval for adolescents.

## Prozac normalizes the brain

How does Prozac affect the adolescent brain? **Neuroplasticity** explains the effects. Neuroplasticity refers to "the brain's ability to reorganize itself in response to the environment over the lifespan" (www.medterms.com). The assumption underlying neuroplasticity is that as behavior changes, there must also be a corresponding change in the neural circuitry that produces behavior (Kolb, Gibb, & Robinson, 2004).

An experiment using **fMRI** investigated the brains of twenty-one healthy adolescents and nineteen adolescents diagnosed with depression aged eleven to eighteen (Tao, et al., 2012). If Prozac is approved for adolescent use, then researchers need to know how it works.

The study lasted for eight weeks. Participants watched fearful faces while fMRI scans were collected at the start and the end of the study. After the baseline scans, the adolescents with depression took Prozac for eight weeks.

Baseline fMRI readings showed that adolescents with depression had higher brain activation in the frontal, temporal, and limbic cortexes. After eight weeks, the brain scans of adolescents with depression looked the same as the brains of healthy adolescents. These three brain regions were no longer hyperactive. In addition, the amygdala, a brain region associated with emotions, showed heightened activity as participants with depression looked at the fearful faces. Amygdala activity returned to the level shown in healthy participants after eight weeks on Prozac.

Note to the teacher:

> Use the Tao study about **Prozac** and neuroplastic changes in the brain for the Paper 1 learning outcome "Discuss two effects of the environment on physiological processes." Since the study uses **fMRI**, it is also useful for the learning outcome "Discuss the use of brain imaging technology in investigating the relationship between biological factors and behavior."

A body of research showing neuroplastic changes after taking Prozac needs replication with different samples.

Next, is a discussion about people from nonwestern cultures taking pharmaceutical medications made in the West. What are the benefits and consequences? Remember that **culture** affects all aspects of treatment, even affecting responses to medication (Kleinman, 2004).

## Culture and antidepressants: The example of Japan

Antidepressants can be effective, but an antidepressant is not always a clear solution. What happens when **antidepressants** are used in nonwestern cultures? The increasing use of antidepressants in Japan is a chance to consider the positive and the negative aspects of exporting western drug treatments to nonwestern cultures.

Note to the teacher:

> One consequence of taking antidepressants to Japan may be the end of adaptive **gene-culture co-evolution**, discussed in chapter 7. Evidence is mounting that traditional cultures buffer groups with greater genetic risks.

Antidepressants were rarely used in Japan before 2001 and then dramatically increased (Kirmayer, 2002).

What explains the surge in use? Does the use of antidepressants help more people get needed treatment or does taking antidepressant drugs conflict with the values of traditional Japanese culture?

Japan has a tradition of using drug treatments for physical and mental health other than antidepressants. In addition, Japan offers more mental health services than most Asian countries. So the problem was not a reluctance to use biomedical treatments. *The reluctance was specific to antidepressants.*

Antidepressants had a small market in Japan until 2001. After 2001, SSRI use increased to the equivalent of 25,000,000 U.S. dollars every month.

Depression symptoms exist in Japan. So why did it take so long for antidepressant drugs to become popular? Kirmayer identifies many factors.
1. Historically, Japanese psychiatry focused on severe disorders.
2. The Japanese view distress as physical symptoms.
3. The Japanese government requires new efficacy trials using Japanese samples before any drug is approved for use.
4. Cultural variations in the social meaningfulness of a group of symptoms are important.
5. Values related to relationship harmony and conformity define the Japanese view of the self.

Let's talk a little about each.

Historically, severe psychotic disorders were the focus of Japanese psychiatry and treatment took place in hospital settings. This emphasis contributed to the **stigma** of mental illness throughout Japan.

Japanese persons with depressive symptoms preferred to see internal medicine doctors for physical complaints to reduce stigmatization and conform to social norms. Although 20% of patients seen by clinicians meet the category criteria for depression, Japanese doctors have traditionally prescribed anti-anxiety drugs or just told patients to relax.

Laws about testing drugs in Japan complicate matters. Government policy requires new experiments using Japanese samples before drug approval. Culture affects responses to drug treatments, so it makes sense to require new testing. RCTs are hard to conduct in Japan for many reasons, one being the stigma of participation. Zoloft was not approved for use in Japan because efficacy trials were unsuccessful. As a result, antidepressants were not as widely available as they were in the West.

Between traditions of doctoring in Japan, the problem of stigma, and the difficulty of running efficacy trials, it is not surprising that antidepressant use in Japan got off to a slow start.

Despite these factors, *cultural variation is the key to understanding the reluctance of the Japanese to use antidepressants*. Each culture has a set of socially meaningful values that defines groups of symptoms. The historical practice of treating depressive symptoms as anxiety reflects values of traditional Japanese culture and influences how a set of symptoms are classified by physicians.

The DSM-IV and the ICD-10 reflect socially meaningful ways of classifying a set of symptoms in the West. Is the category "major depression" meaningful to the Japanese? While younger Japanese psychiatrists now promote antidepressants, cultural values keep them from widespread use. Consider the issues. First, mental disease is generally less prevalent in the Japanese than in westerners, perhaps because westerners are more preoccupied with themselves. In contrast, the Japanese focus on interrelatedness and do not want their behavior exaggerated, so sedative drugs are more popular than antidepressants.

Studying the issues *challenges the notion that diagnosing and treating depression is universal.*

Is the reluctance to use antidepressants in Japan simply their failure to adapt to modern times or is it an expression of traditional culture?

Before taking an SSRI, a person in the West may be sad and say, "I am depressed," meaning general unhappiness.

Antidepressants make a person more outgoing and extroverted, an **individualist** view of the self. Japan is a **collectivist** culture, and value harmony and conformity. Taking an SSRI might make the individual stand out, something not valued in Japan. In addition, the Japanese tend to view mood disturbance as social or moral problems.

Sri Lanka provides another example, where many people meet the western diagnostic category of depression. However, their Buddhist point of view prevents disability. To a Buddhist, depressive symptoms can show one's wisdom. Antidepressants interfere with the meditations that transform the self to the ultimate goal of enlightenment.

The consequences can be great for a culture when individuals take antidepressants. The World Health Organization's Nations for Mental Health Program promotes drug treatments throughout the world, supported by drug companies. To what extent is the promotion of biomedicine beneficial?

Kleinman (2004) also asks questions about exporting western biomedical treatments and writes, "The professional culture, driven by the political economy of the pharmaceutical industry, may represent the leading edge of a worldwide shift in norms" (p. 2). The shift in **norms** comes with benefits and consequences.

## Biomedical Treatment #2: Exercise is just as effective as drugs

**Exercise** is an effective depression treatment. Exercise alters the brain and many of the changes are similar to brain changes after taking drugs (Nahas & Sheikh, 2011). Exercises releases **neurotransmitters** such as **serotonin**, promotes growth in the **hippocampus**, and lowers **cortisol**, an important human stress hormone. In addition, exercise provides social connections and helps people feel in control of their health. Some doctors hesitate to prescribe exercise because of low patient motivation, but it is recommended as a first line of defense for all patients if doctors provide a structured exercise routine and check on progress with counseling.

Exercise is as effective as drug treatments (Babyak et al., 2000). Participants continuing to exercise after ten months of treatment had fewer depression relapses than participants taking medication.

Researchers recruited 156 experiment participants aged fifty and older interested in exercise. All met the DSM-IV requirements for major depression.

Participants were randomly assigned to one of three groups. The first group received three aerobic exercise sessions each week for sixteen weeks. The second group took Zoloft, an SSRI. The third group took both the exercise program and Zoloft.

Depression symptoms were measured at the start of treatment, at the end of the sixteen-week period, and six months after the end of the experiment, for a total of ten months.

All three groups showed similar remission rates at the end of the sixteen week period, 60.4% for the exercise group, 65.5% for the medication group, and 68.8% for the combined group. The most interesting results were those after six months. After the full ten-month period, those who exercised reported lower depression rates than those taking medication, even participants taking medication along with an aerobic program.

Exercise is a valuable depression treatment. The researchers considered reasons for the exercise group's success. People who responded to study advertisements were more likely to show negative attitudes toward drug treatments. Some of the participants in the combined group said the drug interfered with the exercise. Exercise may increase **self-efficacy** for mastering a task, and taking a drug at the same time as exercising interferes with priorities. Expectations for improvement were also likely, as participants were motivated enough to respond to an advertisement about exercise.

It is impossible to know if maintaining an exercise program between the end of the original sixteen weeks and the six month follow-up period *caused* continued depression relief. Participants may have exercised because they were less depressed. The authors speculate, "these results suggest a potential reciprocal relationship between exercise and depression: feeling less depressed may make it more likely that patients will continue to exercise, and continuing to exercise make it less likely that the patient will suffer a return of depression symptoms" (p. 637).

## Biomedical treatment #2: Exercise helps maintain depression treatment

A growing body of research suggests that exercise is just as effective as drug treatments and helps maintain treatment progress over time.

Original data from the SMILE showed that Zoloft and exercise were just as effective in lessening depressive symptoms in a correlation study (Hoffman, et al., 2011). The SMILE study was an experiment where participants were randomly assigned to receive Zoloft, supervised aerobic exercise, home-based exercise, or a drug placebo. The exercise groups performed as well as the Zoloft group, and 44% of both groups showed significant decreases in depressive symptoms. Participants were free to choose any treatment they wished during a one-year follow-up period.

The aim of this follow-up study to SMILE was to find out if continued Zoloft or an exercise program was most effective in maintaining treatment progress.

Self-reports about exercise routines and continued drug use were collected and correlated with the treatment choice and depressive symptoms after one year. Some participants selected just exercise or a combination of exercise and Zoloft.

Results showed that 66% of participants showed fewer depressive symptoms after one year and it was correlated only to exercise.

The authors believe that continued exercise after initial treatment extends the benefits of primary exercise programs and build on the benefits of taking Zoloft.

## Biomedical treatment #3: Acupuncture is an effective depression treatment

**Acupuncture** is a **Traditional Chinese Medicine** (TCM) treatment where fine needles are inserted into acupuncture points connecting to meridians, the electrical channels circulating throughout the body. Acupuncture restores energy, or Chi, flow throughout the body.

Acupuncture affects physiology in many ways, such as releasing **neurotransmitters** and reducing pain (Nahas & Sheikh, 2011). Poorly designed studies plagued early acupuncture research. Some studies did not use control groups. In addition, **placebos**, or **sham acupuncture**, have a physical effect that complicates testing the use of real acupuncture points. Previous studies using placebo acupuncture often confused the physiological response from the placebo with the treatment response because the placebo needles were inserted too close to the real acupuncture needles.

New experiments fix the problems and show that both **laser acupuncture** and **electroacupuncture** are effective. Laser acupuncture does not use needles. Instead, a laser device that looks like a pen stimulates acupuncture points. Electroacupuncture uses needles inserted at desired acupuncture points that are attached to a device providing a small and continuous electrical current to all the needles.

Acupuncture does not hurt, contrary to first impressions of people new to TCM. Needles are hair thin and not at all like the needles used for flu shots or sewing. Patients often cannot feel the needles. Laser acupuncture does not use needles and is a good choice for studying placebo effects because the person does not feel any stimulation. Instead, the patient just knows the laser pen is pressing the point but may not get any stimulation in the placebo condition. The electrical current used in electroacupuncture is not a shock. Its purpose is to provide consistent stimulation to acupuncture points. Acupuncture is very relaxing.

## Two acupuncture experiments

Side effects are one reason people stop taking antidepressants, so it is important to find alternatives that act like antidepressants but do not have the side effects. The first experiment used **fMRI** to examine brain changes during **laser acupuncture** or a placebo condition (Quah-Smith, et al., 2012). The authors predicted that laser acupuncture would cause the same brain changes as antidepressants.

Ten depressed participants received both laser acupuncture and placebo acupuncture while the fMRI watched the brain.

Results showed that laser acupuncture was more effective than a placebo and include the following.

1. Laser acupuncture makes brain regions active similar to the brain activation that occurs after taking antidepressants, such as switching on the medial frontal gyrus, which is often deactivated in people with depression.
2. Laser acupuncture creates quiet time in the brain, referred to as "**yoga time for the brain**," by modifying its resting state activity, or what the brain does when not performing a task. The brain still works in a resting state and acupuncture makes the down time meditative.
3. Laser acupuncture adjusts **cerebellum** activity, which is associated with mood regulation and emotion perception.

Ten participants is a small sample, but the data is high quality and part of a growing body of research showing that acupuncture is more effective than placebos in treating depression.

The second experiment asked if **electroacupuncture** combined with **Prozac** made the drug work faster (Zhang, et al., 2012). Antidepressants are often ineffective when used alone, so it is important to search for **eclectic**, or combinations of treatments, therapies using natural remedies without side effects.

The sample consisted of seventy-three patients with major depression who were randomly assigned to receive a combination of electroacupuncture/Prozac or placebo acupuncture/Prozac. The electroacupuncture group received treatment to acupuncture points in the forehead.

Results showed that participants receiving electroacupuncture in combination with Prozac had significantly faster improvement than participants in the placebo/Prozac condition. Electroacupuncture appears to enhance Prozac's results.

## Individual Treatment: Cognitive therapy (CT)
*Cognitive therapy attempts to bring negative automatic thoughts to conscious awareness*, explained in chapter 7. The therapy focuses on present perceptions of events and the automatic distortions that are applied to the events. The therapist challenges the client to examine the validity of automatic thoughts. A large body of research shows that CT is beneficial for persons with depression and is relevant cross-culturally. CT is the most studied psychotherapy and is frequently compared to drug treatments or combined with them.

## Cognitive therapy study #1: CT is effective for severely depressed persons
Cognitive therapy (CT) is well studied, particularly for people with mild and moderate symptoms. Might cognitive therapy be as effective as an antidepressant for people with severe symptoms? Cognitive therapy was compared to antidepressant drugs in a randomized placebo controlled experiment, and many participants had severe and constant symptoms (DeRubeis, et, al., 2005).

The 240 participants meeting DSM-IV diagnoses for depression were randomly assigned to one of three groups.

Groups received Paxil, a drug placebo, or CT. Treatment lasted for sixteen weeks for the Paxil and CT groups, but for ethical reasons, placebo treatment ended after eight weeks, long enough to see differences between it and Paxil.

The experiment took place at two sites, Vanderbilt University and the University of Pennsylvania.

Data on symptom reduction were gathered at the end of eight weeks for all three groups and then at sixteen weeks for CT and Paxil. At the end of eight weeks, 50% of the Paxil group, 43% of the CT group, and 25% of the placebo group showed positive symptom reduction. At the end of sixteen weeks, there was no overall significant difference between the Paxil and CT groups when data from both sites were combined. The results differed depending on the site, and only data from Pennsylvania showed that drugs and CT had similar effectiveness.

The authors conclude that both moderate and severe cases respond better to drugs and CT than a placebo. The different findings from the Vanderbilt and Pennsylvania sites were probably related to therapist skill. Future research must ensure that all therapists are well trained. Results do not support American Psychological Association and National Institute of Mental Health (NIMH) recommendations that severely depressed patients automatically need drug treatments. The authors conclude that when administered by a qualified therapist, CT is just as effective as drugs for severely depressed patients.

## Cognitive therapy study #2: CT and antidepressants target different depression symptoms

New research clarifies when to use a treatment. Might cognitive therapy and antidepressants help patients with moderate to severe symptoms in different ways (Fournier, et al., 2013)? Both cognitive therapy and antidepressants can be effective, and now health professionals can match patients to treatments that best target specific symptoms.

Participants with depression were randomly assigned to one of three groups, cognitive therapy, Paxil, or a placebo. Comparisons were made within each group to see if the assigned treatment was best based on the following symptom clusters.
1. Anxiety
2. Mood
3. Cognition/suicide
4. Vegetative-atypical
5. Typical-vegetative

Don't get overwhelmed by the psychiatric language. Vegetative symptoms are related to sleeping, eating, weight loss, and experiencing pleasure. Atypical does not mean unusual. Atypical symptoms are more common in women and refer to symptoms starting early in life, having constant symptoms, over sleeping, and hypersensitivity to interpersonal rejection.

Results included the following.
1. Paxil made a faster change in cognitive or suicide symptoms compared to a placebo at four weeks. Both Paxil and CT were effective after eight weeks.
2. Cognitive therapy made a faster change in atypical-vegetative symptoms compared to a placebo.

Drugs and cognitive therapy have different general pathways to help patients and *the future of treatments involves matching patients to treatments*. Drugs and cognitive therapy did not reduce symptoms better than the placebo for the other three clusters. For example, depressed mood and loss of interest are part of an overall diagnosis, but the placebo worked just as well in the study for those specific symptoms.

In conclusion, patients might get treatments tailored to their symptoms in the future.

## Culture and cognitive therapy for depression

Cognitive therapy is cross-culturally relevant as long as therapists understand the **etics** of counseling theory and **emic** features of a person's cultural context. Etics refer to aspects of a therapy that are universally beneficial, such as the way that a therapist establishes a relationship with a client (Kenny, 2006). Emic approaches apply the therapy in culturally meaningful ways, such as using a culture's specific way of problem-solving in counseling sessions.

Case studies support cross-cultural applications of CT. The case of Andrea, a thirty-seven year-old Seminole Native American Indian, is an example. Andrea's treatment was **eclectic**, including CT, antidepressants, Alcoholics Anonymous (AA), client centered therapy, and behavioral therapy. While Andrea's combination treatment included client centered and behavioral therapies, they *supplemented* CT, antidepressants, and AA. Sensitivity to Andrea's cultural background was important throughout the therapy.

Andrea's case adds something valuable to the scant research available on treating depressive symptoms in Native American Indians.

Andrea had many stressors, such as her grandmother's and brother's death, her adolescent daughter's pregnancy, a difficult divorce, a new relationship, and staying away from alcohol. Andrea reported many symptoms, such as headaches, excessive worrying, inferiority, anxiety, fatigue, low energy, and fear of losing control. Andrea met the DSM-IV requirements for Major Depression.

Kenny treated Andrea in forty-nine sessions over twenty-two months.

Andrea's primary treatment consisted of CT, antidepressants, and AA. Client centered therapy techniques, such as active listening and reflection of feeling, were used throughout the forty-nine sessions for support. Behavioral therapy consisted of assertiveness training and was added three months into the treatment to help Andrea set limits on taking responsibility for others, especially her daughter, and attend to her own needs. The behavioral therapy helped Andrea develop cognitive rehearsal strategies to cope with everyday life demands.

Andrea made numerous changes. She started a new relationship, coped better with her daughter, reported improved mood, and stopped taking antidepressants. It took a long time for Andrea to share her cultural values. For example, it took several months for Andrea to discuss a cultural event, a corn dance. It may take a long time to develop a productive client-counselor relationship with persons outside of western culture. In particular, Native American Indians are unlikely to share sacred practices with a therapist early in treatment.

Kenny warns that *case studies are unique to an individual*, so Andrea's treatment plan cannot be generalized to all Native American Indians with depressive symptoms.

Case studies are non-experimental. It is unknown if Andrea's eclectic treatments caused her changes. Second, future research about cross-cultural applications of CT must take into account the different ways that persons display cognitive distortions.

## Group treatment: Mindfulness based cognitive therapy (MBCT)

Group **mindfulness based cognitive therapy** (MBCT) reduces the risk of relapse after depressive symptoms are in remission by combining the best of cognitive therapy and meditation theory (Teasdale, et al., 2000). MBCT is *not* recommended as a primary treatment for depression.

Note to the teacher:

> I recommend the film "Alternative Therapies: A Scientific Exploration: Meditation (2008), available from the Films for the Humanities and Sciences. It reviews early MBCT and other studies, such as Sarah Lazar's brain imaging studies about how meditation changes the brain. Lazar's research is also relevant for the Paper 1 learning outcome about the effects of the environment on physiology.
> 
> The film shows early efforts at quantifying meditation. New studies since the film have expanded the research base for meditation and health, so this film is an introduction to the topic and outlines early studies.
> 
> Students studying the health option are required to evaluate strategies for coping with stress, so the material has another use.

Relapse after depression treatment is common and costly. Antidepressants stabilize depression symptoms, but patients do not need to take them indefinitely. Could MBCT as a follow-up therapy keep patients stable after symptom remission?

MBCT is cost effective when offered as a *group skills training program*. MBCT providers believe that just a small amount of low mood is enough to trigger negative thinking after completing primary treatment.

MBCT is different from CT. CT aims to change the content or meanings of thoughts. MBCT involves learning to *disengage* from thinking, where thoughts are reframed as "mental events" (p. 616). Thoughts are just thoughts, and do not always represent reality. People learn to acknowledge the existence of thoughts or emotions without having them trigger the negative associations that start a relapse. MBCT gives people a different way to relate to their thoughts and emotions.

The experiment aimed to show that MBCT was effective in teaching people to disengage from negative mood and thoughts. The sample consisted of 145 depressed patients in remission from major depression. Participants were randomly assigned to receive treatment as usual (TAU) or to attend MBCT training. Participants assigned to the TAU condition could consult their family doctor or get any other help they would normally choose if symptoms returned. The MBCT program was delivered in eight weekly sessions, each lasting two hours. Participants completed homework between sessions, such as listening to guided meditations and applying new skills to everyday life.

Key parts of MBCT training are *empowerment* and *an open and accepting response* to all thoughts and emotions. Participants learned they had a choice to no longer automatically accept and react to negative thoughts and emotions as they did in the past. The analogy of driving on a familiar road and "of suddenly realizing that one has been driving for miles 'on automatic pilot' unaware of the road or other vehicles, preoccupied with planning future activities or ruminating on a current concern" (p. 618) was helpful to describe automatic responses to thoughts and emotions. MBCT teaches "mindful driving" where one is fully conscious of each moment and responds without the shackles of old habits.

Results showed that relapse rates of participants in MBCT were 50% less than the relapse rates of participants in the TAU condition. The effectiveness was strongest for participants with three or more episodes of depression. The authors speculate that persons with three or more episodes are most likely to have relapses triggered by negative thoughts.

The findings were replicated by Ma and Teasdale (2004). MBCT is an effective and cost efficient way to prevent relapse in persons with three or more depressive episodes.

## Group treatment: A cross-cultural experiment about group interpersonal therapy (IPT) with adolescent war survivors

Paul Bolton's experiment about group IPT therapy for depression relates to the IB course in four ways. First, it is an experiment evaluating group therapy. Second, it is an example of how a therapy developed in the West, IPT, is relevant cross-culturally. Third, it relates to a human relationships learning outcome titled "Discuss the effects of short-term and long-term exposure to violence." One affect of long-term exposure to violence *is an increased risk of mental illness*, including depression and anxiety. Fourth, the experiment evaluates an anxiety disorder treatment.

The Ugandan war was violent and long lasting, with about 1.8 million people, particularly ethnic Acholi, displaced over twenty years of fighting (Bolton, et al., 2007).

Participants were fourteen to seventeen year-old Acholi adolescents who were internally displaced because of war and lived in one of two camps in Northern Uganda.

Adolescents were selected for the study based on the results of the Acholi Psychosocial Assessment Instrument (APAI). The APAI was developed to study locally defined depression-like and anxiety-like disorders that are similar in many, but not all ways, to the DSM-IV categories. Depression-like symptoms were created by combining the definitions of three categories of locally defined behaviors. One category is *Par*, which includes "Has lots of thoughts, wants to be alone, is easily annoyed, holds head, drinks alcohol, and has lots of worries" (p. 520). Another category is *Two Tam*, which includes "Experiences body pain, feels that brain isn't functioning, and thinks of self as being of no use" (p. 520). The last category is *Kumu*, which includes "Has loss of appetite, feels pain in the heart, does not sleep at night, and feels cold" (p. 520). The APAI included anxiety-like symptoms. The local population used the term *Ma Lwor*, meaning "Clings to elders, constantly runs, dislikes noise, has fast heart rate, and thinks people are chasing him/her" (p. 520).

IPT was selected because of the strong experimental research supporting its effectiveness as an individual depression treatment. IPT was designed in the 1970s to treat depression (Hecker & Thorpe, 2005). IPT examines past and current social roles and assumes that mental illness occurs within a social system. One's social, or interpersonal, roles are keys for recovery.

In addition to IPT, a creative play (CP) condition was offered. CP's goal was to strengthen **resilience** through creative verbal and nonverbal activities.

Participants were randomly assigned to receive group IPT, CP, or to a waiting list for sixteen weeks.

Results showed that participants in the IPT group had a significant reduction of depressive-like symptoms over the waiting list controls. When data were analyzed by **gender**, the significance differences were just for girls. Those in the CP group showed no significant depressive-like symptom reduction over the waiting list controls. Further, anxiety-like symptoms failed to improve in either IPT or CP.

IPT effectively treats depression symptoms in girls displaced by war. Boys may be less willing to share emotions in group settings. Although depression symptoms in girls were significantly reduced, neither girls nor boys improved in day-to-day life situations right after the study. The authors note that daily life skills may improve after time passes and that experiment data just measured success by immediate symptom reduction.

# Chapter 12

# Discuss the use of eclectic approaches to treatment

**Eclectic** approaches to treatment combine two or more therapies to enhance treatment.

Sometimes health providers have a primary orientation but supplement it with other treatments. One eclectic treatment is an antidepressant combined with cognitive therapy. Another eclectic treatment is acupuncture combined with antidepressants.

## Advantages of using an eclectic approach

Advantages of using an eclectic approach include the following:

1. Eclectic approaches have a broader theoretical base and may be more sophisticated than approaches using a single theory (Lebow, 2003).
2. Eclectic approaches offer clinicians greater flexibility in treatment. Individual needs are better matched to treatments when more options are available (Lebow, 2003).
3. The newest research shows that one treatment can work faster when combined with a second, such as

acupuncture aiding antidepressants (Zhang, et al., 2012).
4. Sometimes a primary treatment is necessary to stabilize a patient, and the combination treatment is meant to extend treatment progress and help the patient build skills to maintain health. For example, antidepressants might be necessary to stabilize a patient, but cognitive therapy or exercise create long-term health.

## Limitations of using an eclectic approach
Some disadvantages of eclectic approaches include the following:

1. Can researchers always know which treatment worked?
2. Sometimes clinicians use eclectic approaches in place of a clear theory. Eclectic approaches are not substitutes for having a clear treatment theory (Lebow, 2003).
3. Sometimes eclectic approaches are applied inconsistently. It takes knowledge and skill to deliver eclectic approaches effectively (Lebow, 2003).
4. Sometimes eclectic approaches are too complex for one clinician to manage. Coordinating treatment efforts can be challenging (Lebow, 2003).

## Eclectic example #1: Antidepressants and Cognitive Therapy for depression
Use the three TADS studies discussed in chapter 11.

# Eclectic example #2: Antidepressants and acupuncture for depression

Use the Zhang, et al., (2012) experiment discussed in chapter 11.

# Chapter 13

# Discuss the relationship between etiology and therapeutic approach in relation to one disorder

Modern models of etiology are more complex than older models. Depression is the primary example, but the same ideas apply to treating any mental illness.
1. No one treatment works for everyone. Even if a primary etiology is found, the selected therapeutic approach should take into account a client's cultural values, their ability to tolerate drug treatments, their enthusiasm for group therapy, their willingness to change negative cognitive style, and their self-efficacy to start and follow through with the lifestyle changes necessary for exercise treatments.
2. Identifying a specific "cause" of any mental disorder is difficult. Causation is more realistically interpreted as an interrelated group of factors. *One risk factor is not enough to cause any disorder.* The more risk factors, the greater the risk of mental illness. Besides, correlation studies are the main research method used to investigate etiologies in humans, showing relationships and not causation.
3. Treating "symptoms" is still possible even when causes are unknown. For example, antidepressants

or cognitive therapy treats depressive symptoms. Many clinicians measure symptoms before and after treatment with assessment instruments such as the Hamilton Rating Scale and the Beck Depression Inventory. Many consider a treatment to "work" if the symptoms are reduced. Just keep in mind that not everyone agrees with this definition of "work." For example, TCM practitioners do not think that treating "symptoms" is enough for real-life effectiveness, even if they use symptom reduction in short-term experiments.

4. A primary therapeutic approach is frequently aimed at reducing the greatest risk factor. The greatest risk factor varies by person, and might be lack of exercise, cognitive style, or Chi imbalance.
   *Genetics is not the greatest risk factor.* Genetics are predispositions that increase one's risk of developing a disorder. Students thinking that advances in genetic engineering will end mental illness need to think through the ethical implications of that view. Genes do not determine complex behavior. The best therapeutic approaches for someone with the risk alleles for depression might be those reducing stress. Although drug therapies reduce symptoms for many persons, the drugs do not improve one's stress management. Cognitive therapy or treatment involving lifestyle changes may help someone reactive to stress acquire greater coping skills.

5. Treat the cause if it is known. For example, sedentary patients might benefit from exercise if the health provider suspects exercise is a primary contributor to depression.

6. **Culture** affects beliefs about "causes" and treatments. Reread the material on gene-culture co-evolution in chapter 7 and the material on depressive symptoms in China in chapter 5. How do people living in traditional Japanese culture manage "depressive" symptoms? Does the answer to this question change your view of how to treat depression in nonwestern countries? Second, cultural values affect what is viewed as disordered. For example, the Bagandan of Uganda do not think that many of the "symptoms" labeled mental illness in the West are illnesses requiring medical treatment.
7. **Gender** affects causation. Depression or eating disorder diagnoses may not take into account the way males and females express the disorders. Beliefs about etiologies and treatments may reinforce **stereotypes**.
8. **Eclectic** treatments may be the best approach when more than one etiology of a disorder is known.

Take a tentative approach to addressing these issues. Use the existing studies in this book for support.

# Chapter 14

## To what extent do biological, cognitive, and sociocultural factors influence abnormal behavior?

Biological, cognitive, and sociocultural factors influence abnormal behavior, and *the influence is interactive*. Use the bidirectional model explained in chapter 1 to show the interaction. The best examples come from studying etiologies, meaning factors contributing to the disorder.

### Examples of the interaction

Persons with two short alleles of the 5-HTT gene are more reactive to stressful life situations and have a greater risk of depression (Caspi, et, al., 2010). Polymorphisms, or variations of genes, are important, though not the entire story. Genes unfold in stressful environments, and researchers can show the interaction between the gene and the environment in gene-environment correlation studies. Showing the actual importance of genes is now possible, but the gene does not work alone to produce depression.

Similarly, genes contribute to anorexia, but do not work alone. Genes unfold within environments and chapter 8 discusses genetic research showing the interactions. Cognitive factors, such as perfectionism, and sociocultural factors, such as media, are two important contributors, shown to interact with genetic predispositions.

Check the chapter on etiologies of depression and anorexia for specific examples.

# Chapter 15

# Evaluate psychological research relevant to the study of abnormal behavior

## Guiding points for evaluating research
Consider the following when evaluating research.

1. Many researchers recommend replication or additional research testing different variables or using different samples.
2. Pay attention to *who is included in the sample* when studying treatments. Experiments usually exclude participants not meeting strict criteria and use opportunity samples. Researchers must control experimental samples so that experiments test the treatments and not participant characteristics. Everyone knows that real life patients are "messier" and more complex than study participants. Health care providers must have a way to identify the best treatments.
3. Human studies about etiology, meaning risk factors, are primarily correlation studies.
4. To what extent do concepts created and studied in the West apply cross-culturally? Look for cross-cultural verification of western theories and findings. All psychological concepts must be **etics**,

or universal concepts, to be relevant (Triandis & Suh, 2002).
5. It is impossible to know if any treatment works in the long run. It might depend on how one defines "working." Experiments test treatments over short time spans, such as twelve to sixteen weeks, so they measure short-term effects. Confounding variables interfere with running longer experiments. The TADS studies of Prozac in adolescents uses questionnaires for a one-year follow-up from short-term experiment results, and does not show causation.
6. It is hard to know which therapies are better than others because no study compares all available treatments across all types of patients.
7. The different biomedical treatments, individual cognitive therapy, and group therapies have different assumptions.

# References

Abbo, C, Okello, E. S., Musisi, S., Waako, P., & Ekbad, E. (2012). Naturalistic outcome of treatment of psychosis by traditional healers in Jinga and Iganga districts, Eastern Uganda- a 3 and 6 months follow up. *International Journal of Mental health Systems,* 6: 13, 1-11. retrieved from http://www.ijmhs.com/content/6/1/13.

Abbo, C., Ekbad, E., Waako, P., Okello, E. S., & Musisi, S. (2009). The prevalence and severity of mental illnesses handles by traditional healers in two districts in Uganda. *African Health Sciences,* 9 (1), 16-22. retrieved from www.pubmed.gov.

Alegria, M., Woo, M., Cao, Z., Torres, M., Meng, X., & Striegel-Moore, R. (2007). Prevalence and correlates of eating disorders in Latinos in the United States. *International Journal of Eating Disorders*, 40:S15-S21.

American Psychiatric Association. (2013). Diagnostic and Statistical Manual of Mental Disorders, Fifth Edition. Washington, D.C., American Psychiatric Publishing.

American Psychiatric Association, (2000). Diagnostic and Statistical Manual of Mental Disorders, Fourth Edition, Text Revision. Washington, D.C., American Psychiatric Association.

Arger, C., Sanchez, O., Simonson, J., & Mezulis, A. (2012). Pathways to depressive symptoms in young adults: Examining affective, self-regulatory, and cognitive vulnerability factors. *Psychological Report,* 111(2): 335-348.

Australian Academy of Science (2006). Epigenetics—beyond genes. *Nova Science in the News.* www.scienceorg.au/nova/098/098key.htm.

Babyek, M., Blumenthal, J. A., Herman, S., Khatri, P., Doraiswamy, et, al. (2000). Exercise treatment for major depression: maintenance of therapeutic benefit at 10 months. *Psychosomatic Medicine,* 62, 633-638. Retrieved 3/11/08 from www.psychosomaticmedicine.org/cgi/reprint/62/5/633.

Becker, A. E., Fay, K. E., Khan, A. N., Striegel-Moore, R. H., & Gillian, S. E. (2011). Social network media exposure and adolescent eating pathology in Fiji. *The British Journal of Psychiatry*, 198(1): 43-50. doi: 10.119/bpi.110.078675.

Becker, A. E., (2007), Culture and eating disorders classification. *International Journal of Eating Disorders,* 40, S111-S116.

Becker, A.E., Burwell, R.A., Gilman, S.E., Herzog, D.B., & Hamburg, P. (2002).Eating behaviors and attitudes following prolonged exposure to television among ethnic Fijian adolescent girls. *British journal of Psychiatry,* 180, 509-514.

Belmaker. R. H. & Agam, G. (January 3, 2008). Mechanisms of disease: major depressive disorder. In *The New England Journal of Medicine.* 358, 55-68.

Berry, J. (1969). On cross-cultural comparability. *International Journal of Psychology*, 4: 2, 119-128.

Bolton, P., Bass, J., Betancourt, T., Speelman, L., Onyango, et al. (2007). Interventions for depression symptoms among adolescent survivors of war and displacement in northern Uganda: a randomized controlled trial. *Journal of the American Medical Association*, 298: 5. Retrieved 3/3/08 from www.jama.com.

Book Club/Reading Guides- The Prozac Diary by Lauren Slater. (2008). Retrieved 10/21/08 from www.us.penguingroup.com/static/rguides/us/prozac_diary.html

Butcher, J. N., Mineka, S., I Hooley, J. M. (2007), *Abnormal Psychology and Modern Life*, 13th edition. Boston: Pearson Education, Inc.

Caspi, A., Hariri, A. R., Holmes, A., Uher, R., & Moffitt, T. E. (2010). Genetic sensitivity to the environment: The case of the serotonin transporter gene and its implications for studying complex diseases and traits. *American Journal of Psychiatry,* 167(5): 509-527. doi: 10.1176/appi.ajp.2010.09101452.

Caspi, A. & Moffitt, T. (2006). Gene-environment interactions in psychiatry: Joining forces with neuroscience. *Neuroscience*, 7.

Caspi, A, Sugden, K, Moffitt, T. E., Taylor, A., Craig, I., et al. (July 18, 2003). Influence of life stress on depression: moderation by a polymorphism in the 5-Htt gene. *Science*, 301, 386-389. Retrieved 1/17/08 from www.sciencemag.org.

Castillo. R. J. (1997). *Culture and Mental Health: A Client-Centered Approach.* Belmont, CA: Brooks/Cole.

Chiao, J. Y. & Blizinsky, K. D. (2010). Culture-gene coevolution of individualism-collectivism and the serotonin transporter gene. *Proceedings of the Royal Society,* 277, 529-537. doi:10.1098/rspb.2009.1650.

Chinese Society of Psychiatry (2005). History of Chinese Psychiatry. Retrieved from www.cma-mh.org/English/.

Chinese Society of Psychiatry (2003). CCMD-3. Retrieved from www.cma-mh.org/English/.

DeRubeis, R. J., Hollon, S. D., Amsterdam, J. D., Shelton, R. C., Young, P. R., et al. (April, 2005). Cognitive therapy vs. medications in the treatment of moderate to severe depression. *Archives of General Psychiatry*, 62. Retrieved 3/12/08 from www.archgenpsychiatry.com.

Engler, B. (2007). *Personality Theories: An Introduction,* 7th edition. Boston: Houghton-Mifflin.

Flaws, B. (2003). A clinical audit of the treatment of depression with integrated Chinese-Western medicine. *Blue Poppy Press Recent Research Report #335.*

Retrieved 10/31/08 from www.bluepoppy.com.

Fournier, J. C., DeRubeis, R. J., Hollon, S. D., Gallop, R., Shelton, R. C., et al. (2013). Differential change in specific depressive symptoms during antidepressant medication or cognitive therapy. *Behavior Research and Therapy*, 51: 392-398. retrieved from www.elsevier.com/locate/brat.

Grohol, J. M. (2012, Dec. 14). Final DSM 5 approved by American Psychiatric Association. Retrieved 12/14/12 from http://psychcentral.com.

Hammer, L. (2005). *Dragon Rises, Red Bird Flies: Psychology and Chinese Medicine,* Revised edition. Seattle, WA: Eastland Press.

Harvard Magazine (2000). Worse living through chemistry: the downsides of Prozac. Retrieved 10/23/08 from http://harvardmagazine.com/2000/05/p-the-downsides-of-prozac.html.

Hecker, J.E. & Thorpe, G.L. (2005). *Introduction to Clinical Psychology.* Boston: Pearson.

Hoffman, B. M., Babyak, M. A., Craighead, E., Sherwood, A., Doraiswamy, et al. (2011). Exercise and pharmacotherapy in patients with major depression: One-year follow up of SMILE study. *Psychosomatic Medicine,* 73: 127-133. doi: 10.1097/PSY. 0b013e31820433a5.

Horwitz, A. (2005). The age of depression. *Public Interest.*

Retrieved 12/8/08 from http://findarticles.com.

Insel, T. (2013, April 29). Transforming diagnosis. National Institute of Mental Health. Retrieved 5/8/13 from www.nimh.nih.gov/about/director/2013/transforming-diagnosis.shtml.

Jabr, F. (2012). Redefining mental illness: Psychiatry's diagnostic guidebook gets its first major update in 30 years. The changes may surprise you. *Scientific American Mind*, Vol. 23, Number 2.

Kaptchuk, T. (1983). *The Web That Has No Weaver: Understanding Chinese Medicine.* Chicago: Congdon & Weed.

Keel, P. K., Brown, T. A., Holm-Denoma, J. & Bodell, L. P. (2011). Comparison of DSM-IV versus proposed DSM-5 diagnostic criteria for eating disorders: Reduction of eating disorders not otherwise specified and validity. *International Journal of Eating Disorders,* 44 (6): 553-560. doi: 10.1002/eat.20892.

Keel, P. (2005). *Eating Disorders.* Upper Saddle River, N.J.: Pearson Prentice Hall.

Kemmer, S. (February/March, 2007). Sticking point. *Scientific American Mind,* 18: 1, 65-69.

Kenny, M. C. (2006). An integrative approach to the treatment of a depressed American Indian client. *Clinical Case Studies*, 5, 37. Retrieved 10/10/08 from www.sagepublications.com.

Kirmayer, L. J. (2002). Psychopharmacology in a globalizing world: the use of antidepressants in Japan. *Transcultural Psychiatry*, 39, 295. Retrieved 10/10/08 from www.sagepub.com.

Kleinman, A. (2012, April 18). The art of medicine: Culture, bereavement, and psychiatry. *The Lancet,* Vol. 379 p. 608-9.

Kleinman, A. (September 2, 2004). Culture and depression. *The New England Journal of Medicine*, 31: 10. Retrieved 3/11/08 from http://coe.stanford.edu/curriculum/courses/ethmedreadings06/em)601garcia1.pdf

Kolb, B., Gibb, R., & Robinson, T. E. (2004). Neuroplasticity and behavior. In Lerner, J, & Alberts, A. E., Eds. *Current Directions in Developmental Psychology.* Upper Saddle River, NJ: Pearson Prentice Hall.

Lam, L. T., & Peng, Z. (2010). Effect of pathological use of the Internet on adolescent mental health. *Archives of Pediatric Adolescent Medicine.* 164 (10): 901-906. doi: 10.1001/archpediatrics.2010.150.

Lambert, K. (2008). Depressingly easy. *Scientific American Mind*, 19(4), 31-37.

Lebow, J. L. (2003). Integrative approaches to couple and family therapy. In Sexton, T. L., Weeks, G. R., & Robbins, M. S., Eds. *Handbook of Family Therapy.* New York: Routledge.

Lee, S. & Kleinman, A. (2007). Are somatoform disorders changing with time? The case of neurasthenia. *Psychosomatic Medicine*, 69: 846-849. doi: 10.1097/PSY.0b013e1815b0092.

Lee, S. (2000). Eating disorders are becoming more common in the East too. *British Medical Journal*, 321, 10-23.

Lee, S., Ho, T.P., & Hsu, L.K. (1993). Fat phobia and non-fat phobic anorexia nervosa: a comparative study of 70 Chinese patients in Hong Kong. *Psychological Medicine*, 23, 999-1017.

Ma, S. H., & Teasdale, J. D. (2004). Mindfulness-based cognitive therapy for depression: replication and exploration of differential relapse prevention effects. *Journal of Consulting and Clinical Psychology*, 72: 1, 31-40. Retrieved 1/20/09 from www.mbct.com.

Makino, M., Tsuboi, K., & Dennerstein, L. (2004). Prevalence of eating disorders: a comparison of western and non-western countries. MedGenMed: *Medscape General Medicine*, 6: 3. Retrieved 10/19/08 from www.pubmedcentral.nih.gov/articlerender.fcgi?artid=143625.

Marsella, A. J., & Yamada, A. M. (2007). Culture and psychopathology: foundations, issues, and directions. In, Kitayama, S. & Cohen, D., Eds. *Handbook of Cultural Psychology.* New York: The Guilford Press.

Marques, L., Alegria, M., Becker, A. E., Chen, C., Fang, A., et al. (2011). Comparative prevalence, correlates of impairment, and service utilization for eating disorders across US ethnic groups: Implications for reducing ethnic disparities in health care access for eating disorders. *International Journal of Eating Disorders*, 44(5): 412-42. doi: 10.1002/eat.20787.

Mazzeo, S. E., & Bulik, C.M. (2009). Environmental and genetic risk factors for eating disorders: what the clinician needs to know. *Child & Adolescent Psychiatric Clinics North America*, 18: 1, 67-82.

Michl, L. C., McLaughlin, K. A., Shepherd, K., & Nolen-Hoeksema, S. (2013). Rumination as a mechanism linking stressful life events to symptoms of depression and anxiety: Longitudinal evidence in early adolescents and adults. *Journal of Abnormal Psychology,* 122 (2): 339-352. doi: 1037/a0031994.

Morrison, C. M. & Gore, H. (2010). The relationship between excessive Internet use and depression: a questionnaire-based study of 1319 young people and adults. *Psychopathology*. 43 (2): 121-6. doi: 10.1159/000277001.

Nahas, R. & Sheikh, O. (2011). Complementary and alternative medicine for the treatment of major depressive disorder. *Canadian Family Physician*. 57: 659-663.

National Institute of Mental Health (2008). Depression. Retrieved from www.nimh.nih.gov/.

Nolan-Hoeksema, S. (2004). Gender differences in depression. In Oltmanns, T. F. & Emery, R. E., Eds. *Current Directions in Abnormal Psychology*. Upper Saddle River, NJ: Pearson Prentice Hall.

Okello, E. S. & Ekblad, S. (2006) Lay concepts of depression among the Baganda of Uganda: a pilot study. *Transcultural Psychiatry*, 43: 2, 287-313. Retrieved 10/1/08 from www.sagepub.com.

Parker, G., Gladstone, G., & Chee, Q. T. (2001). Depression in the planet's largest ethnic group: the Chinese. *American Journal of Psychiatry,* 158:857-864. Retrieved 9/30/08 from http://ajp.psychiatryonline/cgi/content/reprint/158/6/857.

Patel, V., Flisher, A. J., Hetrick, S., & McGorry, P. (2007). Mental health of young people: A global public-health challenge. *Lancet,* 369: 1302-13. doi: 10.1016/ S1040-6736(07)60368-7.

Peele, S. & DeGrandpre, R. (1995, July). My genes made me do it. *Psychology Today,* 28. Retrieved February 4, 2005 from questia.com.

Quah-Smith, I., Wei Wen, B. E., Chen, X., M., et. al, (2012). The brain effects of laser acupuncture in depressed individuals: An fMRI investigation. *Medical Acupuncture*, 24 (3): 161-171. doi: 10.1089/acu. 2011.0870.

Rosenhan, D. (1973). *On being sane in insane places.*

Retrieved May 5, 2009 from http://web.coc.edu/ lminorevans/on_being_sane_in_insane_places.htm.

Sapolsky, R. M. (2004). *Why Zebras Don't Get Ulcers, 3rd edition*. New York: Henry Holt and Company.

Small, G, & Vorgan, G. (2008). Meet your iBrain: how the technologies that have become part of our daily lives are changing the way we think. *Scientific American Mind*, 19: 5, 42-49.

Southgate, L., Tchanturia, K., & Treasure, J. (2008). Information processing bias in anorexia nervosa. *Psychiatry Research*, 160, 221-227.

Tabassum, R., Macaskill, A., & Ahmad, I. (2000). Attitudes toward mental health in an urban Pakistani community in the United Kingdom. *International Journal of Social Psychiatry*, 46: 3, 170-181. Retrieved 11/9/07 from http://isp.sagepub.com.

Tchanturia, K., Harrison, A., Davies, H., Roberts, M., Oldershaw, et al. (2011). Cognitive flexibility and clinical severity in eating disorders. *PLoS One* 6 (6): e20462. doi: 10.13171/journal.pone.0020462.

Teasdale, J. D., Segal, Z. V., Williams, J. M. G., Ridgeway, A., Soulsby, J. M., et al. (2000). Prevention of relapse/recurrence in major depression by mindfulness-based cognitive therapy. *Journal of Consulting and Clinical Psychology*, 68: 4, 615-623. Retrieved 1/20/09 from www.mbct.com.

Torgovnick, K. (2012, Sept. 11). TED Blog: Some stats on the devastating impact of mental illness worldwide followed by some reasons for hope. Retrieved 5/9/13 from http://blog.ted.com/2012/09/11/some-stats-on.

Trace, S. E., Baker, J. H., Penas-Lledo, E., & Bulik, C. M. (2013). The genetics of eating disorders. *Annual Review of Clinical Psychology*, 9: 589-620.

Triandis, H. C. & Suh, E. M., (2002). Cultural influences on personality. *Annual Review of Psychology,* 53: 133-160.

Truax, P. (2001). Review: group psychotherapy is effective for depression. *Evidence-Based Mental Health*, 4: 82. Retrieved 11/12/08 from EBMH Online.

World Health Organization (2001). *World Health Report, 2001.* Retrieved from www.who.org.

World Health Organization (2004). Prevalence, severity, and unmet need for treatment of mental disorders in the World Health Organization world mental health surveys. *Journal of the American Medical Association*, 291: 21. Retrieved 10/8/08 from www.jama.com.

Zhang, Z., Man, S. C., Li, T. Y. J., Wong, W., et al. (2012). Dense cranial electroacupuncture stimulation for major depression- A single-blind, randomized, controlled study. *PLoS ONE,* 7 (1). e29651. doi: 10.1371/journal.pone.0029651.

Made in the USA
Lexington, KY
11 June 2014